SOURCES

Letters

from

Irish People

on Sustenance

for the Soul

EDITED BY
MARIE HEANEY

**TOWN
HOUSE
DUBLIN**

First published in 1999 by

Town House and Country House
Trinity House, Charleston Rd
Ranelagh, Dublin 6

ISBN: 1-86059-104-3

A CIP catalogue record for this book is available from the British Library.

Typeset by Typeform Repro

Cover design by Jason Ellams

Printed in Ireland
by ColourBooks Ltd

Cover image: 'Mrs K' by kind permission of the artist, Howard Hodgkin

SOURCES

CONTENTS

FOREWORD

I asked the contributors to this book what it was that gave them spiritual sustenance. I knew even as I signed the letters that this was a difficult and risky request. As the answers started to come back I became more and more aware of just *how* difficult my request had been. Many of the correspondents expressed difficulties in defining what 'spiritual' meant and others admitted disquiet and an understandable reticence about disclosing such deeply private matters. As I began to appreciate fully how much courage and consideration my correspondents had committed to addressing the question, I became increasingly rueful. But my ruefulness was soon outstripped by gratitude that the question had led to such wealth of material, to such an outpouring of authentic feeling, honestly and eloquently expressed.

As is to be expected, the source of spiritual sustenance varies from individual to individual so the actual material is diverse and wide-ranging. Although a number of the contributors rely on the written word – poetry, drama, aphorisms and traditional prayers – others are inspired or comforted by the beauties of the natural world and others still by music and the visual arts.

The range of emotional response is as diverse as the material. Anger, joy, peace, stoicism, passion and compassion all find their way into the pages of this book. There are thoughtful re-affirmations of orthodox Christianity side by side with rigorous reappraisals of it. There are chronicles of journeys away from the beliefs of childhood, towards individual credos comprising other religions, or towards an abandonment of faith in any form of organised religion. But whatever their position, all of the contributors testify to an inner life that needs sustaining, especially at times of crisis.

This integrity of feeling finds expression in writing of a high quality. In some cases the powerful responses evoked by the question result in letters that are marked by passion and intellectual rigour. In other cases a gentler note of acceptance is sounded. A number of contributors use literature as a spring-board for their own spiritual investigations, displaying great insight and critical ability as they do so. Most of the pieces encapsulate the wisdom that is the hallmark of an examined life.

Since starting to edit *Sources* I have found myself reflecting more and more on the replies that are contained in the book. I have been challenged by the intellectual courage of some of those replies and comforted and confirmed by the wisdom and compassion of others.

A number of the pieces contain phrases so memorable that I find myself repeating them as if they were mantras. They have entered my consciousness in much the same way as the contributors' offerings had entered theirs. The wheel has come full circle and this book has become a source of spiritual sustenance for me.

Marie Heaney
Editor

xi

ACKNOWLEDGEMENTS

For permission to reprint copyright material, the editor and publisher are grateful to the following:

Little, Brown for 'Caged Bird' by Maya Angelou; John Murray (Publishers) Ltd for 'Ireland with Emily' by John Betjeman; Farrar Straus and Giroux for 'The Moose' from *The Complete Poems 1927–1979* by Elizabeth Bishop, © 1979, 1983 by Alice Helen Methfessel; Heinemann Educational Publishers, a division of Reed Educational & Professional Publishing Ltd for the extract from *A Man for All Seasons* by Robert Bolt; The Women's Press Ltd for the extract from *Gorilla My Love* by Toni Cade Bambara, first published in Britain by The Women's Press Ltd, 1984, 34 Great Sutton Street, London EC1V OLQ; Weidenfeld and Nicolson, The Orion Publishing Group, for the extract from *River Out of Eden: A Darwinian View of Life* by Richard Dawkins; Anvil Press Poetry for 'Prayer' by Carol Ann Duffy from *Mean Time* (1993); The Rungstedlund Foundation for extracts from 'Barua a Soldani' in *Shadows on the Grass* by Isak Dinesen (Karen Blixen), © 1960 by Isak Dinesen; Faber and Faber Ltd for the extract from *Four Quartets* by T.S. Eliot; Random House UK on behalf of Robert Frost for 'The Runaway' from *The Poetry of Robert Frost,* edited by Edward Connery Lathem, published by Jonathan Cape; Faber and Faber Ltd for 'Requiem for the Croppies' and 'Villanelle for an Anniversary' from *Opened Ground: Selected Poems 1966-1996* by Seamus Heaney, © 1989 by Seamus Heaney; Uitgeverij Balans on behalf of Unieboek BV for the extract from *An Interrupted Life: The Diaries of Etty Hillesum 1941-1943* by Etty Hillesum; Routledge, London, for 'The Hermit' from *A Celtic Miscellany: Translations from the Celtic Literatures*, © Kenneth Hurlstone Jackson, 1951, 1971; John Johnson Ltd on behalf of Bloodaxe Books Ltd for 'Warning' from *Selected Poems* by Jenny Joseph; the trustees of the Estate of Patrick Kavanagh, c/o Peter Fallon, Literary Agent, Loughcrew, Oldcastle, Co Meath, Ireland, for 'Peace', 'Canal Bank Walk', 'Advent', 'In Memory of My Mother' by Patrick Kavanagh; Peter Kavanagh for 'In Memory of My Mother' from *The Complete Poems of Patrick Kavanagh*, New York, 1996, edited and with commentary by Peter Kavanagh, © 1972, 1996 Peter Kavanagh; Bloodaxe Books Ltd for 'I See You Dancing Father' by Brendan Kennelly from *A Time for Voices: Selected Poems 1960-1990* (1990); Faber and Faber Ltd for 'Epilogue' in *Day by Day* by Robert Lowell, © 1977 by Robert Lowell; Simon and Schuster, Inc. for 'The Watergaw' from *Collected Poems of Hugh MacDiarmid* by Hugh MacDiarmid, © 1948, 1962 by Christopher Murray Grieve; Penguin Books Ltd for 'On Angels' from *The Collected Poems 1931-1987* by Czeslaw Milosz, (Viking, 1988), © Czeslaw Milosz Royalties Inc, 1988; Salmon Publishing Ltd, Co Clare, Ireland for 'Beannacht' in *Echoes of Memory* by John O'Donohue (first published 1994, reprinted 1997), © 1994 by John O'Donohue; W.W. Norton & Company, Inc. for the excerpt from *Twenty One Love Poems* by Adrienne Rich; W.W. Norton & Company, Inc. for 'The Swan' by Rainer Maria Rilke, translated by M.D. Herter Norton, translation copyright by W.W. Norton & Company Inc.; The Hogarth Press for the excerpt from *Duino Elegies* by Rainer Maria Rilke, translated by J.B. Leishman/Stephen Spender; Curtis Brown on behalf of Sir Wilfred Thesiger for the extract from *Arabian Sands* by Sir Wilfred Thesiger, © Wilfred Thesiger, 1984; William Heinemann, Publisher, for the extract from *Cannery Row* by John Steinbeck; Shambhala Publications, Inc., Boston, for the extract from *Song of Myself* by Walt Whitman edited by Stephen Mitchell, © 1993; A.P. Watt Ltd on behalf of Michael B. Yeats for 'The Coming of Wisdom', 'The Ballad of Father Gilligan' and 'Memory' from the *Complete Poems* by W.B. Yeats.

Every effort has been made to trace copyright holders. The publishers apologise for any errors or omissions in the above list and would be grateful to be notified of any corrections that should be incorporated into the next edition of this volume.

KATHY SHERIDAN

Dear Marie Heaney

Your brief was mercifully broad and so – as you will see – is my interpretation of it. But I hope it corresponds somewhat...

I arrived in the small, country town of Omagh within hours of the bomb of August 15th, 1998 and immediately felt like an interloper; a useless stranger to the traumatised, injured and bereaved; a parasite there only to find an angle on their grief. To shed tears seemed fraudulent and self-indulgent and yet I – and many other journalists – often found ourselves overwhelmed by images and stories of suffering beyond human endurance. They were days when some of us questioned our calling and our worth.

It took the stricken people of Omagh to remind us of the possibilities of faith and redemption; of how in moments of agony and near-despair, the ordinary can be rendered extraordinary; of how a simple act of kindness to a stranger could trigger healing and renewal.

For me, that spirit was exemplified by a gentle and ecumenical soul called Michael Gallagher. Here was a man who had just lost his beloved only son but who was able to summon up the Christ-like insight and generosity to lay his two broad hands on my shoulders and say: 'You and your colleagues have come to watch with us in our agony as surely as any of our friends and neighbours... I have seen that in all of you.'

Michael Gallagher is a man whose faith was never dented by his terrible loss. In times of great catastrophe, I am constantly struck by people's cleaving to their God when reason suggests that they should turn their backs on Him. For me, Omagh demonstrated that the fierce need to believe in an afterlife and reunion with loved ones is only a part of it. For these tormented people, like Christ, the overwhelming need was to pray and to believe that their suffering was not in vain, that through the enormity of their grief, wisdom and redemption must surely dawn and grow.

During those weeks in August and for months afterwards, a passage from Aeschylus ran a loop around my brain:

> Pain that cannot forget
> falls drop by drop
> upon the heart
> until in our despair
> there comes wisdom
> through the awful
> grace of God.

The late Bedouin King, Hussein, began his political life by witnessing the assassination of his chief (his grandfather), and ended it by weeping over the bodies of the children of his enemies.

It is a simple and ultimately comforting truth: Man grows wise against his will.

Regards
Kathy Sheridan

CIARAN CARTY

Dear Marie
Here as promised is the piece for your book.

Best wishes
Ciaran

Vaya con Dios

There is a term 'out of body experience' referring to that sensation – of awe, of exhilaration, of rejoicing – which patients are said to recall after they come back from a state of being 'technically dead'. It might equally apply to flying.

You sit strapped to a seat in a fragile tube of aluminium hurtling at 500 mph through the ice-cold atmosphere 30,000 feet above the ground. A vast ocean of rumpled white cloud stretches beneath you broken only by the orange–blue vastness of the early morning horizon, its arc tracing the only just perceptible curvature of the earth. What greater reminder both of the genius of man and of his insignificance. How utterly small and vulnerable you feel in face of the sheer immensity of space and the awesome beauty of nature. Yet how easy to accept it as something by now almost banal, a routine aspect of commuting in modern technological society. Business executives sit in aisle seats – advance-booked to save valuable seconds on arrival – and tap urgent figures on their laptops. A stewardess offers breakfast of fruit, rasher, sausage and pudding – and would you like champagne?

As a teenager, the German composer Karlheinz Stockhausen was assigned to an ambulance crew that helped get the war wounded to hospital. He remembers trees spattered with shreds of human flesh after strafing by planes. His mother suffered deep depression and was incarcerated in a mental hospital where she was officially killed by the Nazis. He feels his belief in the divine has been enhanced by the horrors of his childhood. Out of this spirituality has come some of the

most innovative and inspired music of the 20th century,
beginning with his experiments in Paris using natural sounds
as notes and then with the breakthrough of the first ever
totally electronic musical work *Studie 1* in 1953. He hears
music everywhere and perhaps nowhere more than when he
is flying – literally in the heavens.

Here is Stockhausen after a flight to Dublin: 'Never have I
seen,' he tells me, 'as I saw this morning such a beautiful
composition of small clouds, very small compact clouds with
very irregular shapes and different thicknesses, their
whitishness contrasting with the bluish colours between
them. I cannot make such beautiful silently flying sounds as
the clouds which are made by God. But it has a lot to do with
my music, where sounds and silences and the proportions
between sounds and silences become what you hear.'

With the realisation that while you are in the air your life is
completely out of your own hands comes a palpable sense of
spiritual release (if you can get over being scared witless). A
fragile air-conditioned turbo-prop cocoon protects you like a
reassuring womb. You are born again and strangely at one
with creation. Flying to London often once, sometimes twice a
week – and back in the same day – if anything, enhances the
sensation. It is like visiting a chapel of stillness and
forgiveness.

If it is a clear morning, as the plane glides down to land its
shadow runs before it across the fields and houses until
finally the two become one and you are reunited with that
other self you left behind for the 50 or so minutes of the flight.
For just that brief while your life has been a prayer.

CAHAL DALY

Dear Marie

I am happy to accept your invitation to participate in the book.

The piece which I offer is based on a distinct section of the Book of Isaiah in the Bible, and I accompany this with a statement of the reasons why this text gives me particular spiritual sustenance.

I am glad that the royalties will be given to Focus Ireland. I think that this is a most interesting project, and I wish it every success.

A part of the Bible from which I draw particular spiritual sustenance is that part of the Book of Isaiah which scholars call 'Deutero-Isaiah' or Second Isaiah. It consists of chapters 40–55 of that book. The date of this part of Isaiah is at least 150 years later than that of the first 39 chapters; and its author is a prophet whose name is unknown, but whom, for convenience, we simply call Second Isaiah. He spoke his prophecies mainly to the exiled Jews who had been deported by Nebuchadnezzar, King of Babylon, and who were then living in exile. Nebuchadnezzar had attacked Jerusalem first in the year 597 BC, and taken the king and the royal family into captivity. After an attempted revolt of the Jews against the imperial power of Babylon, Nebuchadnezzar attacked the city again in 587 BC; and this time the city was sacked. The sack of Jerusalem was complete, and it included the total destruction of the Temple. The entire population was deported to Babylon. The deportation and subsequent exile marked a decisive turning point in the history of Israel. It will be remembered that Matthew's Gospel begins with the genealogy of Jesus, in which three periods are distinguished in the history of the Jews: the first from Abraham to David, the second from David to the deportation to Babylon, the third from the deportation to the birth of Jesus Christ.

The deportation and the exile marked the lowest point in the fortunes of the Israelites since their arrival in the Land of Israel. The glories of the Kingdom of David, who ruled, as Psalm 71 puts it, 'from sea to sea, from the Great river to earth's bounds' had ended in humiliation and defeat. The peace and opulence of the reign of Solomon were now the theme of sad songs and national mourning and lament. When *taunted by their Babylonian masters and asked to sing 'one of Sion's songs', the Jews could only reply:*

> Oh how could we sing
> the song of the Lord on alien soil?
> If I forget you, Jerusalem,
> let my right hand wither.

From PSALM 136

The plaintive song of the exiles still rings across the millennia:

> By the rivers of Babylon
> there we sat and wept
> remembering Sion.
> By the poplars that grew there
> we hung our harps.

From PSALM 136

This psalm gives us some idea of the broken heart and spirit of the exiled Jews. Their self-confidence as a race was shattered. Their hopes for a better future for the nation were crushed. Where were the promises of the Lord now? Even their faith in God, their 'everlasting rock', was in danger of crumbling. The trust which they had placed in God, the God of their fathers, was sorely tested. The Covenant to which their sacred books had assured them that God would be 'faithful for a thousand generations and forever' seemed to have been repudiated. The Temple, dwelling place of the Holy One of Israel, the very heart's core of their faith, was a heap of rubble.

A series of psalms expresses the people's lamentation for the ruined temple and their bewilderment that God could have allowed this to happen. 'Where is your God?' the pagans taunted them. One of the psalms of the exile expresses their trial of faith:

> I will say to God, my rock,
> 'Why have you forgotten me?
> why do I go mourning,
> oppressed by the foe?'

From PSALM 41

This psalm was often in the hearts and on the lips of Jews two and a half millennia later, during the holocaust, when again the taunts came, sometimes from unbelieving fellow-Jews: 'Where was God in Auschwitz? ... How can you believe in God after Auschwitz?' As a modern writer puts it, the Jews in exile were 'a people discouraged, dazed and destitute, severely tempted to apostasy'.

It was to such a people that the Second Isaiah spoke in the name of God, as only a prophet could. The first Isaiah had chastised them in God's name for their sinful ways, had called them, sometimes sharply, to penitence, had reminded them, sometimes severely, of God's justice and had warned them solemnly of God's just wrath if they did not repent and return to the Lord.

But now that they had been brought to their lowest ebb, the Jews needed to be given consolation, healing and hope, hope of a new future, a future of peace, when all would be made new. God assured them, through the prophet, that he was about to 'do a new deed on the earth' (Isaiah 43: 19). The prophet of Second Isaiah is God's messenger of comfort to a people in desolation; he is God's messenger of hope to a people in despair.; he is God's word of love to a people who felt abandoned, forgotten and unloved. He is the restorer of faith to a people who were at risk of losing the faith of their fathers and mothers. Appropriately, the Second Book of Isaiah was called by the Jews the Book of the Consolation of Israel. It begins with the words: '"Console my people, console them," says your God' (Isaiah 40: 1).

These chapters of Isaiah contain some of the most amazing words of tenderness and loving-kindness, of pity and patience and compassion, ever spoken by God to His people. Indeed, these are among the most beautiful words in the whole of religious literature. God assures His people that he shares their pain, he pleads with them to believe in His love for them and, in spite of everything, to believe that He is with them.

During the long and heart-breaking years of conflict in Northern Ireland, I found great inspiration in these chapters of Second Isaiah. I found great consolation in the repeated pledges of God's undying love for His people. I drew hope from His repeated assurances that indeed He was about to do 'a new deed'. When the Belfast Agreement was signed on Good Friday 1998, I, like thousands of others, wept with happiness and with thankfulness; for I felt in a new way the truth of God's assurances of love and recognised the fidelity of His promises, His mercy and His power in the new deed he was doing, the new future He was opening up. I felt that we were indeed seeing 'something never told and witnessing something never heard before' (52: 15). I never cease to be amazed at the tenderness with which God

whispers His love in times of discouragement, and pledges His
faithfulness when persons and institutions we trusted let us down:

> Do not be afraid, for I am with you;
> stop being anxious and watchful, for I am your God.
> I give you strength, I bring you help,
> I uphold you with my victorious right hand. ...
> For I, the Lord, your God,
> I am holding you by the right hand;
> I tell you, 'Do not be afraid,
> I will help you.'
> Do not be afraid, Jacob, poor wee creature,
> Israel, you poor little thing,
> I will help you – it is the Lord who speaks –
> The Holy One of Israel is your redeemer.
>
> 41: 10, 13-14

> Do not be afraid, for I have redeemed you;
> I have called you by your name, you are mine.
> Should you pass through the sea, I will be with you;
> or through rivers, they will not swallow you up.
> Should you walk through fire, you will not be scorched,
> and the flames will not burn you
> for I am the Lord, your God,
> The Holy One of Israel, your Saviour ...
> Because you are precious in my eyes,
> because you are honoured and I love you, ...
> Do not be afraid, for I am with you.
>
> 43: 2–5

> With everlasting love I have taken pity on you
> says the Lord, your Redeemer ...
> For the mountains may depart,
> the hills may be shaken,
> but my love for you will never leave you
> and my covenant of peace for you will never be shaken,
> says the Lord, who takes pity on you.
>
> 54: 10

> Listen to me, House of Jacob,
> all you who remain of the House of Israel,
> you who have been carried since your birth,
> you whom I have carried since the time you were born.

In your old age I will still be the same,
when your hair is grey I shall still support you.
I have already done so, I have carried you,
I shall still support you and deliver you.

46: 3–4

*The future lies with men and women of faith, the men and women
who offer hope:*

How lovely on the mountains
are the feet of one who brings good news,
who heralds peace, brings happiness,
proclaims salvation,
and tells Sion, 'Your God is King.'

52: 7

*It is in this Book of Consolation which is Second Isaiah that we find
the four servant songs, describing the suffering of a mysterious
servant of the Lord, who bears our suffering and carries our sorrows,
the One through whose bruises we are healed and who offers his life
in atonement, the One who by his sufferings will justify many,
taking their faults upon himself (Isaiah 53, see also 42, 49 and 50).
The words of the servant songs, and particularly of Isaiah 53, are
frequently applied to Jesus Christ in the Gospel writings, and are
applied by Christ to Himself in several Gospel passages. It is in
Christ that we find the unique Servant of the Lord, the supreme
expression of God's love for humanity; for 'Greater love no-one has
than this, that a man give up his life for his friends' (John 15: 13);
and that man is God made man and dwelling amongst us. In Him
God's word, spoken through Second Isaiah, is fulfilled to the fullness
of the spirit and of the letter:*

Does a woman forget her baby at the breast
or fail to cherish the child of her womb?
Yet even if she should forget,
I will never forget you.

Look I have branded you on the palms of my hands.

*That is why Second Isaiah has long been one of my great sources of
spiritual sustenance.*

Yours sincerely

✠ Cahal B Cardinal Daly

BERNADETTE MADDEN

Dear Marie

I have a collection of quotations, written on scraps of paper, jostling for space on my studio noticeboard; bits of text jotted down (not always absolutely correctly) from the radio or copied from newspapers and books.

'Gratitude must finally become a burden and make friendship impossible' is there, as is 'What, after all, is a halo, except another thing to keep clean.' And 'Just do it!' is there more than once!

But there are two Biblical quotations that have always played a big part in how I try to live my life: 'Thou shalt love thy neighbour as thyself' and 'Better a dinner of herbs where love is, than a stalled ox and hatred therewith.' They are both almost self-explanatory – love, friendship is important, being there for your friends/neighbours is important (and knowing they'll be there for you), self-respect is very important, worldly goods are sometimes important but never as important as the people you love and who love you.

Bernadette Madden

POLLY DEVLIN

Dear Marie

Thank you for your letter which gave me pause for thought. In a sense whatever happens that sustains me in my actual life is also my spiritual sustenance. Early unhappiness, a feeling of powerlessness, the disappearance of conventional 'religion' from my life and the subsequent realisation that I had to help myself (in all its ambiguous senses) when I was about sixteen years old, meant I had to devise a system of a kind. This I did. Not very adequately, in a sustaining sense, but adequate in an ethical sense; and that early religious training has been its underpinning. I live by a tender conscience. I also believe wholly in karma. What goes around comes around and this serves me in a pragmatic way as did Victorian homilies to another generation like Honesty is the best virtue; so I try to do as I would like to be done by.

For years I led such a busy life. I always read a great deal. Then my daughters were born and this, in terms of the widening of my heart was what might be called a religious experience. Certainly I became a different person from the girl I was.

As I got older I began to read more poetry and I found that poetry spoke to me in a way that religious tracts or teaching never did. Was there ever better reason for anyone to be a reader or a writer than Wordsworth's

> Dreams, books are each a world;
> And books we know
> Are a substantial world, both pure and good.
> Round these, with tendrils strong as flesh and blood
> Our pastime and our happiness will grow.

I find that human voices fired by genius uplifted, singing, does for me what prayer once nearly did. It melts the ice. Certain lines are like a mantra, again as a rosary once was. And certain lines frighten the wits out of me in the way that the concept of hell frightens believers. Listen to Yeats:

Civilisation is hooped together, brought
Under a rule, under the semblance of peace
By manifold illusion: but man's life is thought,
And he, despite his terror, cannot cease
Ravening through century after century
Ravening, raging and uprooting that he may come
Into the desolation of reality…

Auden can do it:

A ragged urchin, aimless and alone
Loitered within that vacancy; a bird
Flew up from his well-aimed stone.
That girls are raped, that two boys knife a third,
Were axioms to him who'd never heard
Of any world where promises were kept
Or one could weep because another wept.

And listening to Keats with his nightingale, and Emily Dickinson, mapping out her icy self-pity touches my soul and sustains it:

I can wade pools of grief
But the least touch of joy breaks up my feet.

The other spiritual nourishment comes from my beginning to relive in the country. This place, so simple, was unattainable though it lay all around me. The sustenance I get from animals, plants, trees, fields is central to my life. At the very centre of this life is a field. It is ten acres and there are about one hundred varieties of flowers and grasses in it. Here is a litany: Creeping Bent, Crested Dog's Tail, Sweet Vernal Grass, Purple Moor Grass, Yorkshire Fog, Heath Grass, Timothy, Reedgrass, Field Horsetail, Common Rush, Hard Rush, Soft Rush, Marsh Thistle, Meadow Thistle, Fleabane, Black Knapweed, Sneezewort, Hairy Sedge, Carnation Sedge, Devil's Bit Scabious, Meadow Vetchling, Bird's Foot Trefoil, Dyer's Greenweed, Betony, Self-Heal and Tormentil, Saxifrage, Ribwort Plantain and Yellow Forget-me-Not.

The field lies like a dream of beauty, striped, flecked, spangled and eyed like a peacock. It is every colour under the sun, a mille-fleur revelation which makes you understand that the tapestries of the Middle Ages, the Lady with the Unicorn *from Cluny, were not an artist's dazzling inspiration of the celestial fields, but an accurate representation of what he saw around him: and of what 400 years later I also saw in my childhood, born as I was in the tail end of a dispensation. But in the intervening years I forgot or had to forget or, like most of us, ceased to believe in what I had seen. I lie in that field, most days in the spring or summer, wet or dry, my bare feet planted on the ground and I feel nature breathing. I get sustenance from this. It is a form of pantheism, no doubt, but I think again of poetry and that great pantheist Wordsworth who brings us into another kind of reality, the opposite of Yeats's desolation:*

> Not in Utopia, – subterranean fields, –
> Or some secreted island, Heaven knows where!
> But in the very world, which is the world
> Of all of us, – the place where, in the end,
> We find our happiness, or not at all!

And what may you ask has happiness to do with spirituality?

Everything, everything. That soulful visionary Blake said: 'A man has a duty to be happy.' And so has a woman.

Love

Polly

MARY O'DONNELL

Dear Marie

What gives me spiritual sustenance swings between a number of variables, like music, the written word and sometimes the handed-down ritual of religious praise. Sometimes formal prayer seems redundant for me, yet at other times it is the only resource available to me. When everything I could ever want seems to be to hand anyway, the natural patterns of being and existence which assert themselves through the seasons definitely connect with my most primitive assured spirituality. Nature, I observe (rather than believe), will have its way around us and in us. So, although often I don't believe in a personal God, I do use the Hail Mary almost spontaneously as a means of fixing my attention on something. When all else fails – when it seems we are impotent in the face of active evil (the recent case springs to mind of the man who injected his own son with infected blood so as to avoid paying child support) I start a couple of Hail Marys. But that's usually in relation to things outside myself.

For myself and because this poem always captures the way in which the force of meditative and on-going spirituality is almost outside and beyond personal control, I always read and re-read Carol Ann Duffy's beautiful, tremulous poem 'Prayer'. It is full of quiet desperation, and yet it urges us to reconcile the self with the self. The truth, she says, is 'a small familiar pain'. Half the time, although we do not always recognise it, we live in a state of needing consolation, of experiencing loss, of yearning for what Duffy calls 'a sudden gift'. In the end prayer happens anywhere, all around us, especially when we cannot pray. And now that I think of it, silence is its own prayer. Sometimes I can't have enough of it.

Good luck with this anthology, I'm delighted to be part of it.

Best wishes
Mary O'Donnell

Prayer

Some days, although we cannot pray, a prayer
utters itself. So, a woman will lift
her head from the sieve of her hands and stare
at the minims sung by a tree, a sudden gift.

Some nights, although we are faithless, the truth
enters our hearts, that small familiar pain;
then a man will stand stock-still, hearing his youth
in the distant Latin chanting of a train.

Pray for us now. Grade I piano scales
console the lodger looking out across
a Midlands town. Then dusk, and someone calls
a child's name as though they name their loss.

Darkness outside. Inside, the radio's prayer –
Rockall. Malin. Dogger. Finisterre.

CAROL ANN DUFFY (1955–)

FRANK McGUINNESS

Dear Marie

Thank you for asking me to contribute. I have so much time for Sr Stanislaus, I would do anything for her.

The texts I turn to are Shakespeare's sonnets. They celebrate the human body and the human mind in all our changes and contrariness, our sorrows and our secrets. If they're holy it's because they are angry and even in despair, they are never resigned. Their hatred of women is hateful, so they are not perfect, and that gives them the edge that saves them from being sacred. They are in no way heroic, but they try to be truthful – that's as good a criterion for prayer – to God, to man, to woman – as any I'd expect.

Love

Frank McGuinness

Sonnet 53

What is your substance, whereof are you made,
That millions of strange shadows on you tend?
Since every one hath, every one, one shade,
And you, but one, can every shadow lend.
Describe Adonis, and the counterfeit
Is poorly imitated after you.
On Helen's cheek all art of beauty set,
And you in Grecian tires are painted new.
Speak of the spring and foison of the year:
The one doth shadow of your beauty show,
The other as your bounty doth appear;
And you in every blessèd shape we know.
     In all external grace you have some part,
     But you like none, none you, for constant heart.

WILLIAM SHAKESPEARE (1564–1616)

MARGARET MacCURTAIN

Bestow on me, O Lord, my God, understanding to know
Thee

PRAYER OF ST THOMAS AQUINAS BEFORE STUDY

Dear Marie

*I came to Thomas Aquinas quite young when I read the story of a
solemn little boy who kept asking 'What is God?' and at the age of
sixteen ran away from a strong-minded mother to join the
Dominican friars in Paris. She wanted him to be a Benedictine monk
in Monte Casino, and in due course to become Lord Abbot. Running
away to attain his heart's desire won my childish approval and much
later when I came across his prayers, I appropriated them for my
desires. I always prayed before important examinations, like the old
Intermediate and Leaving Certificates of the 1940s, and kept up the
custom at university. By that time I knew he possessed one of the
greatest minds of all time but that did not change my affection for the
student who was nicknamed 'the dumb ox' by his supercilious
companions in the University of Paris. His petitions I made my own
and after many years I have not discarded them:*

> Bestow on me, O Lord, my God, understanding to know
> Thee, diligence to seek Thee, wisdom to find Thee, a life
> and conversation which may please thee, perseverence
> in waiting patiently for Thee, and a hope which may
> embrace Thee at the last. Grant me to be pierced with
> compunction by Thy sorrows through true repentance,
> to improve all Thy gifts and benefits during this my
> pilgrimage through Thy grace, and so at length to enter
> into Thy full and consummate joy in Thy glory.

THOMAS AQUINAS

*When I became a teacher I found another bond with this gentle-
hearted scholar who liked to entertain his students with his witty
examples and give them a feast once a year. Thomas Aquinas prayed
that his heart would never grow cold or corrupt. Towards the end of
Ibsen's great play* Peer Gynt, *Peer peels an onion and compares each*

skin with a phase of his life and finally discovers that an onion does not have a heart. Thus he confronts his own heartlessness. I am grateful to Thomas Aquinas for keeping me faithful to my heart by reciting his prayer for his heart:

> Give me, O Lord God, an ever watchful heart, which no subtle speculation may lure from Thee. Give me a noble heart, which no unworthy affection can draw downwards to the earth. Give me an upright heart, which no insincere intention can warp. Give me a firm heart, which no tribulation can crush or quell. Give me a free heart, which no perverted or impetuous affection can claim for its own.

THOMAS AQUINAS

I have kept the best prayer for last. Thomas Aquinas composed the great Eucharistic hymn, 'Adoro Te devote' which does not translate easily and which people who grew up in the first half of the twentieth century recited or sang in Latin. It is a wonderful poem, or hymn, and though not as rapturous or entrancing as the other great hymn, 'Panis Angelicus', it is one of my everyday meditations. Here is the second verse:

> Visus, tactus, gustus in te fallitur,
> Sed auditu solo tuto creditur:
> Credo quidquid dixit Dei Filius,
> Nil hoc verbo Veritatis verius.

THOMAS AQUINAS

The elegant, simple Latin of Thomas Aquinas is lost in translation:

> Sight, touch and taste in Thee are each deceived,
> The ear alone most safely is believed:
> I believe all the Son of God has spoken,
> Than truth's own word there is no truer token.

THOMAS AQUINAS

Best wishes and good luck with the project
Margaret MacCurtain

MARK PATRICK HEDERMAN

Dear Marie

Thank you for inviting me to participate. An interesting question: 'Your personal choice of whatever it is that gives or has given you spiritual sustenance.' I have given a short story by Baroness Karen Blixen (Isak Dinesen) as a parable or symbol of my kind of food.

I have been a Benedictine monk for 35 years now and what you call 'spiritual sustenance' is for monks Lectio Divina *or 'spiritual reading' which we do every day.*

Apart from the Bible, which is sui generis, *but which, as one Jewish commentator has remarked, is as much a bloodcurdling novel for God about us, as it is a theology for us about God, there is a major industry of 'spiritual' books meant to edify and improve the one who 'truly seeks God' as the Benedictine Rule describes the potential monk. This library ranges from guidebooks and manuals of prayer, to, for instance,* The Lily of Israel, *a three volume novel about a little girl who died and went to heaven after making her first communion.*

I found most of these to be hortatory rhetoric, pious platitude or wishful thinking. Certainly not spiritual sustenance. As James Joyce wrote in a letter to his brother Stanislaus: 'I am nauseated by their lying drivel about pure men and pure women and spiritual love and love for ever: blatant lying in the face of truth.' It all seems to be part of a conspiracy to anaesthetise rather than energise.

> 'Blood on the moon, ' they said,
> and I agreed,
> but saw it not
> and yet I pretended to see.
> 'This is,' they said, 'your life.
> Your art and sensitivity
> are naught but furniture for this same hour.'
> 'Sit whisperingly still
> in cold grey dawn:' they said,
> 'this breathless anonymity
> is prayer.'

And only I can say:
'It's not.'
'Not what?'
'Not me!'

I love, like Nietzsche's Zarathustra, 'only that which is written with blood. Write with blood: and you will discover that blood is spirit.' One day, as I browsed through the eclectic, sprawling, unkempt monastic library, a book seemed to fall out of the shelf into my hand. I opened it and began to read. I stood there, riveted and trembling as if I was reading a love letter just delivered through the post-box. It seemed to have been written directly to me; as if I were the only person ever to have read it before. I kept looking over my shoulder in case someone might be eavesdropping on my delirium. What was I understanding? What was being communicated to me? What was this sound? It was the sound of clinking in the darkness, someone with a key outside the door of my cell. Spiritual sustenance, a letter from the king, Lectio Divina.

And Lectio Divina *for three reasons: First because of what you are 'reading'. In some way or other the object of attention is 'inspired'. As in Seamus Heaney's 'Postscript' to* The Spirit Level *(a pun on that presence of the Spirit. The pun being 'two thinks at a time' according to Joyce):*

You are neither here nor there,
A hurry through which known and strange things pass
As big soft buffetings come at the car sideways
And catch the heart off guard and blow it open.

SEAMUS HEANEY (POSTSCRIPT)

In Wahrheit, Singen ist ein andrer Hauch! Ein Hauch um nichts. Ein Wehn im Gott. Ein Wind.

Really singing issues from a different breath. A breath from nowhere. A draught in God. A wind.

RAINER MARIA RILKE (SONNET 3 TO ORPHEUS)

Something more has entered the work. Bergman described it in a television interview with Melvyn Bragg some years ago. He gave three examples from his own work: the death scene in Cries and Whispers, *the seashore in* Sawdust and Tinsel, *the woods in* Wild

Strawberries. *Something more than the actors or actresses or he, as director, had put into the film, actually happened and appeared on the screen. When everyone on the set has given everything and a magic of perfection hits the scene, it is then that the gods throw down fire and something extra is added to perfection.*

Iris Murdoch's last novel, Jackson's Dilemma, *written as Alzheimer's disease, from which she now suffers,*[1] *was about to make all such writing impossible for her, exudes another energy which takes over and allows the novel to describe the process by which the Spirit intervenes in human lives.*

The second 'divine' element is the way it crosses your path. The so-called coincidence, which others give the grander name of synchronicity. Sometimes you receive it in the post or an angel delivers it, or it falls on your head off the shelf. This in my experience is the way the Spirit infiltrates our over-planned lives. 'And no one saw your foot prints, O Lord,' the psalmist says. Doris Lessing calls coincidences God's way of remaining anonymous.

The third is the way it affects you. In all such 'spiritual reading' the first word is an adverb describing an activity, not an adjective qualifying a particular kind of text. It is the Holy Spirit who guides you along the right path, nourishes you with manna, *bread from heaven, food for the desert. In Hebrew manna means 'What is it?' Such food can be of any variety and is different for every person whose path it bestrews. Any bread can be kneaded, tran-substantiated. It becomes as personal as your finger-print, as distinctive as your taste. This is what you have always been looking for, what you need at this moment. 'Give us this day our daily bread.'*

And you know that it is nourishing you, marrowing your bones, doing you good, because you feel it entering your bloodstream, colouring your horizon, energising you. It remains with you and increases like silt on a riverbank as you get more of it, until eventually it grows into what you have become because of it. Such letters from the king provide illumination never before intimated to you and impossible to repeat or articulate exactly, but which remains inside you as self-evident axioms, starting-blocks from which you spring into action from now on. I have found such sustenance in some poems of Seamus Heaney, some plays of Brian Friel, some films

---

1 Editor's note: Iris Murdoch has died since these words were written.

*of Ingmar Bergman, some novels of Iris Murdoch, to mention one
from each. Because of such sustenance I enter my 55th year 'still full
of sap, still green,' as the psalmist teaches me to say, yet again. The
psalms being consummate correspondence between kings.*

Mark Patrick Hederman

from Barua a Soldani

When I first came out to Africa I could not live without
getting a fine specimen of each single kind of African game.
In my last ten years out there I did not fire a shot except in
order to get meat for my Natives. It became to me an
unreasonable thing, indeed in itself ugly or vulgar, for the
sake of a few hours' excitement to put out a life that belonged
in the great landscape and had grown up in it for ten or
twenty, or – as in the case of buffaloes and elephants – for fifty
or a hundred years. But lion-hunting was irresistible to me; I
shot my last lion a short time before I left Africa.

As now on this New Year's morning as noiselessly as possible
I got down from the car and, through the long wet grass that
washed my hands, the rifle, and my face, slowly walked
closer to the lion, he stirred, rose and stood up immovable, his
shoulder towards me, as fine a target for a shot as in the
course of a lifetime you would get anywhere in the world.
The sun by now was just below the horizon, the morning sky
behind the dark silhouette was clear like liquid gold. I was
struck by a thought: 'I have seen you before, I know you well.
But from where?' The answer came at once: 'It is a lion out of
the royal coat of arms of Denmark, one of our three dark-blue
lions on gold ground. *Lion posant or* it is called in the heraldic
language – he knows it himself.' As I sat down on the ground,
got Denys' rifle into position on my knee and took aim, I
made a resolution: 'If I get this lion, the King of Denmark is to
have the skin.'

As the shot fell, booming loudly in the still morning
landscape and echoing from the hills, it looked to me as if the
lion was carried a couple of feet straight upwards into the air
before he came down and collapsed. He had been hit in the
heart, it was as it should be.

Now it fell out that this lion was an exceptionally fine specimen, what out in his own country they call a black-maned lion, with his thick dark mane growing all back over his shoulder-blades. Denys' gun-bearer, who had seen many hundred lion-skins, declared this one to be the finest he had ever come across. And as in that same spring I was going on a visit to Denmark after four years in Africa, I took the skin with me and on my way, in London, gave it to the firm of Rowland Ward to be cured and set up.

When in Denmark I told my friends that I meant to give King Christian X the lion-skin, they laughed at me.

'It is the worst piece of snobbery that we have ever heard of,' they said.

'Nay but you do not understand,' I answered them. 'You have not lived for a long time outside your own country.'

'But what in the world is the King to do with the skin?' they asked. 'He does not mean to appear at New Year's levée as Hercules! He will be in despair about it.'

'Well,' I said, 'if the King will be in despair, he will have to be in despair. But I do not think it need come to that, for he will have some attic at Christiansborg or Amalienborg where he can put it away.'

If the King really was in despair about it he hid it very nobly. Some time after my return to the farm I had a kind letter from him, in which he thanked me for his lion-skin.

A letter from home always means a lot to people living for a long time out of their country. They will carry it about in their pocket for several days, to take it out from time to time and read it again. A letter from a king will mean more than other letters. I got the King's letter about Christmas-time, and I pictured to myself how the King had sat at his writing-table at Amalienborg, gazing out over a white Amalienborg Square with the snow-clad equestrian statue of his great-great-great grandfather, King Frederic V, in a wig and classic armour, in the midst of it. A short time ago I myself had been part of the Copenhagen world. I stuck the letter into the pocket of my old khaki slacks and rode out on the farm.

The farm work that I was going to inspect was the clearing of a square piece of woodland where we were to plant coffee, a couple of miles from my house. I rode through the forest, which was still fresh after the short rains. Now once more I was part of the world of Africa.

Half an hour before I came out to the wood-fellers a sad accident had taken place amongst them. A young Kikuyu, whose name was Kitau, had not managed to get away quick enough when a big tree fell, and had had one leg crushed beneath it. I heard his long moanings while still at a distance. I speeded up Rouge upon the forest path. When I came to the place of disaster Kitau's fellow-workers had dragged him out from beneath the fallen tree and laid him on the grass; they were thronging round him there, separating when I came up but standing close by to watch the effect of the catastrophe on me and to hear what I would say about it.

Kitau was lying in a pool of blood, his leg had been smashed above the knee and was sticking out from his body at a grotesque and cruel angle.

I always had morphia at hand in my house for injured people of the farm carried up there, but here I had neither the medicine nor the syringe. Kitau, when he realized that I was with him, groaned out dolefully: 'Saidea mimi' – help me – 'Msabu.' And again: 'Saidea mimi. Give me some of the medicine that helps people,' the while groping over my arm and knee. When out riding on the farm I usually had bits of sugar in my pockets to give to the totos herding their goats and sheep on the plain and at the sight of me crying out for sugar. I brought out such bits and fed Kitau with them – he would or could not move his badly bruised hands, and let me place the sugar on his tongue. It was as if this medicine did somehow relieve his pain; his moans, while he had it in his mouth, changed into low whimperings. But the stock of sugar came to an end, and then once more he began to wail and writhe, long spasms ran through his body. It is a sad experience to sit by somebody suffering so direly without being able to help; you long to get up and run away or, as with a badly injured animal, to put an end to the anguish – for a moment I believe I looked around for some kind of weapon for the purpose. Then again came the repeated clock-regular moaning of Kitau: 'Have you got no more, Msabu? Have you got nothing more to give me?'

In my distress I once more put my hand into my pocket and felt the King's letter. 'Yes, Kitau,' I said, 'I have got something more. I have got something *mzuri sana*' – very excellent indeed. 'I have got a *Barua a Soldani*' – a letter from a king. And that is a thing which all people know, that a letter from a king, *mokone yake*' – in his own hand – 'will do away with all pain, however bad.' At that I laid the King's letter on his chest and my hand upon it. I endeavoured, I believe – out there in the forest, where Kitau and I were as if all alone – to lay the whole of my strength into it.

It was a very strange thing that almost at once the words and the gesture seemed to send an effect through him. His terribly distorted face smoothed out, he closed his eyes. After a while he again looked up at me. His eyes were so much like those of a small child that cannot yet speak that I was almost surprised when he spoke to me. 'Yes,' he said. 'It is *mzuri*,' and again, 'yes, it is *mzuri sana*. Keep it there.'

When at last the car arrived and we got Kitau lifted on to it, I meant to take my seat at the steering wheel, but at that he immediately worked himself into a state of the greatest alarm. 'No, Msabu,' he said, 'Farah can drive the car, you must tell him to do so. You will sit beside me and hold the *Barua a Soldani* to my stomach as before, or otherwise the bad pain will come back at once.' So I sat on the boards beside him, and all the way into Nairobi held the King's letter in position. When we arrived at the hospital Kitau once more closed his eyes and kept them closed, as if refusing to take in any more impressions. But with his left hand on my clothes he kept sure that I was beside him while I parleyed with the doctor and the matron. They did indeed allow me to keep close beside him while he was laid on the stretcher, carried into the building and placed on the operating table; and as long as I saw him he was quiet.

I may in this place tell that they did really in hospital manage to set his broken leg. When he got out he could walk, even if he always limped a little.

I may also here tell that later on, in Denmark, I learned from the King himself that my lion-skin had obtained a highly honourable place in the state-room of Christiansborg Castle, with the skin of a polar bear to the other side of the throne.

But now the rumour spread amongst the squatters of my farm that I had got this *Barua a Soldani*, with its miracle-working power. They began to come up to my house one by one, warily, to find out more about it – the old women first, mincing about like old hens turning their heads affectedly to find a grain for their young ones. Soon they took to carrying up those of their sick who were in bad pain, so that they might have the letter laid on them and for a while be relieved. Later they wanted more. They demanded to borrow the King's letter, for the day or for the day and night, to take with them to the hut for the relief of an old dying grandmother or a small ailing child.

The *Barua a Soldani* amongst my stock of medicine from the very first was accurately and strictly placed in a category of its own. This decision was taken by the Natives themselves without my giving any thought to the matter. It could do away with pain, in this capacity it was infallible, and no ache or pang could hold out against it. But it must be made use of solely in uttermost need.

It did happen from time to time that a patient with a very bad toothache, in his misery cried out to me to let him have *Barua a Soldani*. But his appeal would be met by his surroundings with grave disapprovement and indignation or with haughty, scornful laughter. 'You!' they cried back to him, 'there is nothing the matter with you but that you have got a bad tooth! You can go down to old Juma Bemu and have him pull it out for you. How could you have the King's letter? Nay, but here is old Kathegu very ill in his hut with long, hard pains in his stomach, and going to die tonight. His small grandson is up here to have *Barua a Soldani* for him until tomorrow from Msabu. To him she will give it.' By this time I had had a

leather bag with a string to it made for the King's letter. So the
small toto, standing up straight on the terrace, would take the
remedy carefully from my hands, hang it round his neck and
walk away, with his own hands upon it. He would stand up
straight on the terrace again next morning. Ay, his
grandfather had died at sunrise, but *Barua a Soldani* had
helped him well all night.

I have still got the King's letter. But it is now undecipherable,
brown and stiff with blood and matter of long ago.

In a showcase at the Museum of Rosenborg, in Copenhagen,
the tourist can see a piece of yellow texture covered with
tawny spots. It is the handkerchief of King Christian IV, which
the King held to his eye socket when, in the naval battle of
Kolberger Heide three hudred years ago, his eye was
smashed by a Swedish shot. A Danish poet of the last century
has written an enthusiastic ode about these proud, edifying
marks.

The blood on my sheet of paper is not proud or edifying. It is
the blood of a dumb nation. But then the handwriting on it is
that of a king, *mokone yake*. No ode will be written about my
letter; still, today it is, I believe, history as much as the relic of
Rosenborg. Within it, in paper and blood, a covenant has been
signed between the Europeans and the Africans – no similar
document of this same relationship is likely to be drawn up
again.

KAREN BLIXEN (1885–1962)

DONNACHA RYNNE

Dear Marie Heaney

Thank you sincerely for the opportunity to give my thoughts. I have been known to write poetry but have not written for a number of years and this might be my opportunity to start afresh.

Dóchas

I have great ability to accept things as they are and to embrace my disabilities and move gracefully through life.

Sometimes I feel isolated and lonely but I get great sustenance from the wild gales of West Clare and I get a good kick when the sand brushes against me as if it is cutting the face off me.

Sometimes I sit and wallow in my frustrations but I let them go, through working with the breath and doing the odd Yoga posture. Music plays a healing role in my life and lifts me out of my frustrations. I like nothing better than to sit and listen to John Spillane, Donal Lunny or Mary Coughlan, light a candle and burn some lavender oil.

One of the things I find extremely difficult is letting my emotions flow. I'm too quick to put on the 'I'm all right Jack' attitude – good old stoic Donnacha! I like to think that my stoicism is fading and that one day I will express my grief.

I love the solitude of where I am living, it gives me great ease of mind and allows me to think clearly. Being near the crashing waves of Spanish Point on a winter's day gives my soul a lift. To say a prayer, to focus on Padre Pio, to sit and meditate by the sea, to be at peace.

Another of the things that has given me sustenance is the wonderful loving and spiritual writings of my grandfather, Stephen Rynne.

In sharing my experience I hope it lifts the spirit of others and gives them positive energy and enthusiasm to express themselves.

Go raibh míle maith agat
Mise, le meas
Donnacha Rynne

KATHLEEN WATKINS

If you believe, as I do, that prayer to a great extent is the expression of the good wishes, loving kindness and agreeable intent towards another person, then if it is a prayer for your mother you seek, you need search no further than John O'Donohue's poem for Josie. It seems to me that the poem encapsulates a great deal of the ancient Celtic attitude to prayer and its expression which he wrote so well about in Anam Chara and other works, which found, not surprisingly, such a ready response from Irish people.

The poem is the epitome of loving, longing for only good things for an adored mother, but I believe that with only a tiny shift of emphasis it can be made to apply to anyone. I regularly read the 91st Psalm with my daughters in mind whenever they are away – it is my prayer for their happiness and well-being and safe return home.

Father John O'Donohue's poem for his mother is not far removed from this.

Kathleen Watkins

Beannacht
for Josie, my mother

On the day when
the weight deadens
on your shoulders
and you stumble,
may the clay dance
to balance you.

And when your eyes
freeze behind
the grey window
and the ghost of loss
gets in to you,
may a flock of colours,
indigo, red, green,

and azure blue
come to awaken in you
a meadow of delight.

When the canvas frays
in the currach of thought
and a stain of ocean
blackens beneath you,
may there come across the waters
a path of yellow moonlight
to bring you safely home.

May the nourishment of the earth be yours,
may the clarity of light be yours,
may the fluency of the ocean be yours,
may the protection of the ancestors be yours.

And so may a slow
wind work these words
of love around you,
an invisible cloak
to mind your life.

JOHN O'DONOHUE (1953–)

MICHEAL O'SIADHAIL

Dear Marie

How nice of you to ask me! But I hardly know how to begin to answer your question. A world so rich and various, all the poems, the novels, the paintings and sculptures, music which I couldn't imagine a life without, quite apart from the excitement of language and science. After much thought, I've chosen an extract from a book which I only discovered a few years ago: An Interrupted Life : The Diaries of Etty Hillesum 1941–43, *by a twenty-seven-year-old Jewish woman in Amsterdam, which first appeared in 1982. As we approach the millennium, I find these diaries particularly moving and appropriate to our time.*

> So many inhibitions, so much fear of letting go, of allowing things to pour out of me, and yet that is what I must do if I am ever to give my life a reasonable and satisfactory purpose. It is like the final liberating scream that always sticks bashfully in your throat when you make love. I am accomplished in bed, just about seasoned enough I should think to be counted among the better lovers, and love does indeed suit me to perfection, and yet it remains a mere trifle, set apart from what is truly essential, and deep inside me something is still locked away.

And there follows eighteen or so months of the most extraordinary entries. This student in the Faculty of Slavonic Languages at the University of Amsterdam, daughter of a classics teacher and a Russian-born Jewish mother, records with a scalpel honesty and passion her doings with her lovers, friends and family. Against the backdrop of the tightening Nazi grip on Holland, she moves between the household of Hans Wegerif, a widower of sixty-two who she had an intimate relation with, and the house of her lover the charismatic Julius Spiers, a fifty-two-year-old Jewish therapist and former student of Jung who had fled Berlin. Her two houses were, as Etty tells us, 'three streets, a canal and a little bridge' apart. Yet, the real distance was from the panicky, introspective, young intellectual to the beautiful and rooted maturity of her final lines: 'We should be willing to act as a balm for all wounds.'

Etty Hillesum refused to escape. After the death of Julius Spiers, she worked in Westerbork Camp to alleviate her fellow-Jews. On September 7th 1943, with her father, mother and her brother, she was sent to Auschwitz. From the train she threw a card found and posted by local farmers: 'We have left the camp singing.'

I think of her diary as compressing into eight exercise books a whole lifetime's growth. But more, it's as if the second half of the twentieth century is squeezed into those barely decipherable lines. Our slow stumbling from desolate individualism towards some repaired notion of freedom as the privilege to serve. Her unblinking testimony and her counteracting joyful vision of humanity both chasten and liberate me. Born just over three years after her death, my life has fumbled along in tandem with this half century. I need her brightness, her wisdom, her strength.

Yours

Micheal O'Siadhail

Extract from the diary of Etty Hillesum 1 July [1942] 3.45 in the afternoon.

Sun on the balcony and a light breeze through the jasmine. As I said a new day has dawned – how many of them have there been since seven o'clock this morning? I shall linger another ten minutes with the jasmine, and then on the household bicycle – for which we have a permit – to see a friend who has been part of my life for sixteen months and whom I feel I have known for a thousand years, yet who can still suddenly present me with an aspect so new that I catch my breath with surprise. How exotic the jasmine looks, so delicate and dazzling against the mud-brown walls.

I can't take in how beautiful this jasmine is. But there is no need to. It is enough simply to believe in miracles in this twentieth century. And I do, even though the lice will be eating me up in Poland before long.

It is possible to suffer with dignity and without. I mean: most of us in the West don't understand the art of suffering and experience a thousand fears instead. We cease to be alive being full of fear, bitterness, hatred and despair. God knows, it's only too easy to understand why. But when we are deprived of our lives are we really deprived of very much? We have to accept death as part of life, even the most horrible of deaths. And don't we live an entire life each one of our days, and does it really matter if we live a few days more or less? I am in Poland every day, on the battlefields, if that's what one can call them. I often see visions of poisonous green smoke, I am with the hungry, with the ill-treated and the dying every day, but I'm also with the jasmine and with that piece of sky beyond my window; there is room for everything in a single life. For belief in God and for a miserable end. When I say I have come to terms with life, I don't mean I have lost hope. What I feel is not hopelessness, far from it. I have lived this life over a thousand times already, and I have died a thousand deaths. Am I blasé then? No. It is a question of living life from minute to minute and taking suffering into the bargain. And it is certainly no small bargain these days. But does it matter if it is the Inquisition that causes people to suffer in one century and war and pogroms in another? To suffer senselessly as the victims would put it? Suffering has always been with us, does it really matter in what form it comes? All that matters is how we bear it and we fit it into our lives. Am I merely an armchair theorist safely ensconced behind my desk, with my familiar books around me and the jasmine outside? Is it all theory, never tested in practice? I don't think so. All our conversations are now interlarded with sentences such as 'I hope he'll still be there to enjoy these strawberries with us.' I know that Mischa, with his delicate physique, has been ordered to report to Central Station and I think of Miriam's and Renate's pale little faces, and of many, many worried people, and I know it all, everything, every moment and I sometimes bow my head under the great burden that weighs down on me, but even as I bow my head I also feel the need, almost mechanically to fold my hands. And so I can sit for hours and know everything and bear everything and grow stronger in the bearing of it, and at the same time feel sure that life is beautiful and worth living and meaningful. Despite everything. But that does not mean that I am always filled with joy and exultation. I am often dog-tired after standing about in queues and I know that this too is part of life and *somewhere there is something inside me that will never desert me again.*

ETTY HILLESUM (1914–43)

FERGAL KEANE

Dear Marie

Thanks for your letter.

I have chosen some lines from Nadezhda Mandelstam, from Hope Abandoned, *written after the final arrest and effective 'disappearance' of her husband, the great poet Osip Mandelstam. She writes to him although she already believes he is dead. On first reading it is one of the most heartbreaking pieces of writing in any language. But read it again and again and feel the power of her love, stretching out across the vastnesses of the Soviet empire to the vanished poet. Whenever I go to war zones I carry with me the works of Osip Mandelstam and Anna Akhmatova; now I also make sure I carry these lines of Nadezhda. Her love, the love braided into every word of every line, is the hope, her love is the spiritual comfort.*

> In my last dream I was buying food for you in a filthy hotel restaurant. The people with me were total strangers. When I had bought it I realized I did not know where to take it, because I do not know where you are. When I woke up I said to Shura: 'Osia is dead.' I do not know whether you are still alive, but from the time of that dream, I have lost track of you. I do not know where you are. Will you hear me? Do you know how much I love you? I could never tell you how much I love you. I cannot tell you even now. I speak only to you, only to you. You are with me always, and I who was such a wild and angry one and never learned to weep simple tears – now I weep and weep and weep. It's me: Nadia. Where are you?
>
> Farewell,
>
> Nadia

And that's it, Marie. Breathtakingly beautiful. Not immediately consoling, in fact desolate on the first reading. But read again and the love sings.

Fergal Keane

AUSTIN FLANNERY

Dear Marie

I wish you every success with the book.

I cannot think of just one piece of writing which, more than any other, sustains me spiritually. There have been books, but I find it difficult to pick out one book, let alone one passage.

If pushed, one of several passages which I could short-list is the magnificent prologue to St John's gospel. The gospel has been described as 'full of insight, feeling and beauty', and this is especially true of the prologue. It sets out many of the gospel's major themes, much as an overture does for a piece of music.

The prologue is capable of releasing one's spirit, sending it soaring aloft. So much of Christian belief and spirit is there, expressed so tranquilly, so contemplatively.

Yours

Austin Flannery OP

In the beginning was the Word, and the Word was with God, and the Word was God. He was in the beginning with God. All things came into being through him, and without him not one thing came into being. What has come into being in him was life, and the life was the light of all people. The light shines in the darkness and the darkness did not overcome it.

There was a man sent from God, whose name was John. He came as a witness to testify to the light, so that all might believe through him. He himself was not the light, but he came to testify to the light. The true light, which enlightens everyone, was coming into the world.

He was in the world, and the world came into being through him; yet the world did not know him. He came to what was his own, and his own people did not accept him. But to all who received him, who believed in his name, he gave power to become children of God, who were born, not of blood or of the will of the flesh, or of the will of man, but of God.

And the Word became flesh and lived among us, and we have seen his glory, the glory as of a father's only son, full of grace and truth. (John testified to him and cried out, 'This is he of whom I said, "He who comes after me ranks ahead of me because he was before me."') From his fullness we have all received grace upon grace. The law indeed was given through Moses; grace and truth came through Jesus Christ. No one has ever seen God. It is God the only son who is close to the Father's heart who has made him known.

PAULA MEEHAN

Greetings, Marie

I get a huge amount of comfort and inspiration from this 10th century text. A millennium has passed and it is as fresh and clear and immediate as the day it was uttered. Though I am not a Christian I identify strongly with this urge to worship, and to be transported by, the experience of the natural world. I've felt the same delight in a city square watching a blackbird worrying the rasher rind an office worker has discarded from her lunch. It's more than a hymn to nature – it's a hymn to the enoughness of the experience of being alive and an enactment of the eternal playful song of the self in nature. 'A beautiful pine makes music to me, it is not hired'. Had they worries about the commodification of art back then? '…will you go with me to see it?' Does our hermit sometimes feel the loneliness of his path and wish for a companion?

Robert Frost, in his great poem, 'Birches', says 'Earth's the right place for love:/ I don't know where it's likely to go better'. I feel that way about spiritual experience – earth's the right place for it. '…pignuts, wild marjoram, the cresses of the stream – green purity!' For sure!

Paula Meehan

The Hermit's Hut

… I have a hut in the wood, none knows it but my Lord; an ash tree this side, a hazel on the other, a great tree on a mound encloses it.

Two heathery door-posts for support, and a lintel of honey-suckle; around its close the wood sheds its nuts upon fat swine.

The size of my hut, small yet not small, a place of familiar paths; the she-bird in its dress of blackbird colour sings a melodious strain from its gable.

The stags of Druim Rolach leap out of its stream of trim meadows; from them red Roighne can be seen, noble Mucraimhe and Maenmhagh.

A little hidden lowly hut, which owns the path-filled forest; will you go with me to see it?…

A tree of apples of great bounty,…, huge; a seemly crop from small-nutted branching green hazels, in clusters like a fist.

Excellent fresh springs – a cup of water, splendid to drink – they gush forth abundantly; yew berries, bird-cherries…

Tame swine lie down around it, goats, young pigs, wild swine, tall deer, does, a badger's brood.

Peaceful, in crowds, a grave host of the countryside, an assembly at my house; foxes come to the wood before it – it is delightful…

Fruits of rowan, black sloes of the dark blackthorn; foods of whorts, spare berries…

A clutch of eggs, honey, produce of heath-peas, God has sent it; sweet apples, red bog berries, whortleberries.

Beer with herbs, a patch of strawberries, delicious abundance; haws, yew berries, kernels of nuts.

A cup of mead from the goodly hazel-bush, quickly served; brown acorns, manes of briar, with fine blackberries.

In summer with its pleasant, abundant mantle, with good-tasting savour, there are pignuts, wild marjoram, the cresses of the stream – green purity!

The songs of the bright-breasted ring doves, a beloved movement, the carol of the thrush, pleasant and familiar above my house.

Swarms of bees, beetles, soft music of the world, a gentle humming; wild geese, barnacle geese, shortly before All Hallows, music of the dark torrent.

A nimble singer, the combative brown wren from the hazel bough, woodpeckers with their pied hoods in a vast host.

Fair white birds come, cranes, seagulls, the sea sings to them, no mournful music, brown fowl out of the red heather.

The heifer is noisy in summer, brightest of weather; not bitter or toilsome over the mellow plain, delightful, smooth.

The voice of the wind against the branchy wood, grey with cloud; cascades of the river, the swan's song, lovely music.

A beautiful pine makes music to me, it is not hired; through Christ, I fare no worse at any time than you do.

Though you delight in your own enjoyments, greater than all wealth, for my part I am grateful for what is given me from my dear Christ.

Without an hour of quarrel, without the noise of strife which disturbs you, grateful to the Prince who gives every good to me in my hut.

Irish; author unknown; tenth century
Trans: K H JACKSON

SEÁN BRADY

Dear Ms Heaney

Choosing a favourite piece of literature is never easy. Eventually it came down to a choice between the two Ulster poets, Seamus Heaney and Patrick Kavanagh. Finally Kavanagh won out, probably because he evokes so powerfully rural life and particularly the drumlin country in the first half of this century, scenes that were very familiar to me as I grew up in east Cavan in the forties and fifties. The nostalgic in me, that longing for things as they once were, brought me to choose 'In Memory of My Mother' by Patrick Kavanagh.

With every good wish,
Yours sincerely,

✠ Seán Brady
Archbishop of Armagh

In memory of my mother
Died November 10th, 1945

You will have the road gate open, the front door ajar
The kettle boiling and a table set
By the window looking out at the sycamores –
And your loving heart lying in wait

For me coming up among the poplar trees.
You'll know my breathing and my walk
And it will be a summer evening on those roads
Lonely with leaves of thought.

We will be choked with the grief of things growing,
The silence of dark-green air
Life too rich – the nettles, docks and thistles
All answering the prodigal's prayer.

You will know I am coming though I send no word
For you were lover who could tell
A man's thoughts – my thoughts – though I hid them –
Through you I knew Woman and did not fear her spell.

PATRICK KAVANAGH (1904–67)

JOHN O'DONOHUE

Dear Marie

I have been travelling a lot and found it hard to find the time and concentration write something. I hope this is alright.

Yours sincerely

John O'Donohue

Mountains: The Earth's Contemplatives

Nature is the oldest scripture. It holds the silent wisdom of the first encounter of light and darkness, earth and water, fire and air. Its primal imagination knows the silence from the time before anything was and the passion of the threshold at which first stones, clay and fire emerged. Nature has an ancient memory. It knows more than the human mind could ever unearth. Long before the human shadow fell across its fields, the Earth celebrated its own liturgy of wind and silence, rain and ocean. The seasons stayed in rhythm knowing their curve through time. The moon swivelled the tides and the shorelines waited. The faith of the Earth is seamless.

In the form of mountains the Earth reached out toward the heavens. Mountains are huge gestures of transcendence. Rooted in eternal time, they stand silent and still in their great solitude. Mountains are the contemplatives of the Earth. Over millions of years they preside in a landscape, absorbing the breath of its plants, the lowing of the animals and returning often the echo of the human cry as if to remind us that Earth is always listening. Mountains have an ancient *uaisleacht* that never wavers.

Connemara is a landscape of bleak and exacting tension; everything is pared down to its Beckettian essence. It is a landscape that depends hugely on light. When the light is present, the whole place glows, incandescent with subtle colour. When the light departs, Connemara falls back into the grip of a dark gravity. This is a landscape that lives on the threshold between light and darkness. There is an ancient conversation going on here between the sky and these bleak fields. The mountains stand between them, ever stately and constant amidst the swirl of moods above and below.

Often during the night the fog comes down. In the morning the mountains are gone. A screen of grey fog hides everything. Sometimes, even mountains need to get away from the burden of visibility. Some mornings the fog has come half-way down a mountain. The top of the mountain has disappeared and the stem of the mountain is rendered lucent and vivid. This is the kind of image the imagination loves: huge presence absolutely adjacent yet hidden from the eye. Without Nature, there would be no imagination. Without the imagination, there would be no Gods. It is good to go out into Nature and linger among its subtle and sublime rhythm to allow the imagination to be schooled in its deft art of silence, stillness and solitude. Made in her image and likeness, our clay selves are deeply at home here. Our invisible minds reach out in longing to mountains. Maybe this is how it began. The poet-carpenter who loved the earth found his vision in the 'lonely places'.

MÁIRE Mhac an tSAOI

Dear Marie

I was thrown by the word 'spiritual' which I no longer seem to understand in its contemporary context. 'In all dangers, temptations and afflictions' to quote the old catechism (which adds 'and when the clock strikes'!), I fall back on the 'Hail Mary'. When I seek the satisfaction of doing what I'm good at, I read and write Irish. Unfortunately, other more practical occupations constantly get in the way of this last, and I spend a large part of my time doing what I'm not good at. Early conditioning, I imagine.

I wish the project every success.

Warm regards

Máire Cruise O'Brien
(Máire Mhac an tSaoi)

Hail Mary, full of grace,
The Lord is with thee.
Blessèd art thou amongst women
And blessèd is the fruit of thy womb, Jesus.

Holy Mary, mother of God,
Pray for us, sinners,
Now and at the hour of our death.
Amen

PATRICIA DONLON

Dear Marie

For most of my life I thought that spirituality could only be achieved by renouncing the earthly – through novenas, rosaries and lots of self-denial. The older I get, the more I believe that to find true spiritual sustenance means becoming firmly rooted in reality, in the here and now. Only through an awareness of this world can we raise ourselves to a higher plane. There are many books that help me make that leap and in trying to decide I have agonised and chosen and then rejected my first selection and started over again. So for today, these are my choice – tomorrow will be a different story.

Ann Morrow Lindberg's Gift from the Sea *has been a constant companion of mine for many years now. Her struggle to maintain her sense of self as she balances her work as a writer with her responsibilities as wife and mother are hauntingly revealed in this small treasure of a book. In each chapter a different phase of her life is symbolised by a series of shells discovered on a beach. Thoughtful, lucid prose and great personal honesty make this a book that women in particular will find inspiring. Then there is Elizabeth von Arnim's* Elizabeth and her German Garden *which this non-gardener finds compulsive reading and which contains much humour and insight. A recent find is Philippe Delerm's* The Small Pleasures of Life *– a series of meditations on the tiny things that make life worth while.*

However, for days when I feel worn-out and shabby like an old toy whose stuffing has fallen out, I read Margery Williams's story for children, The Velveteen Rabbit, *with its beautifully muted illustrations by William Nicholson, and take comfort.*

The Velveteen Rabbit arrived on Christmas morning. The little boy loved him – for at least two hours – but in the excitement of the day he was soon forgotten. For a long time he lived with the other toys in the cupboard – and they were a pretty mixed lot: bossy mechanical toys who were very superior, full of modern ideas and talk of technology. Even the little wooden lion who should have known better pretended that he had connections with Government. The

Velveteen Rabbit felt very insignificant. The only person to be kind to him was the old Skin Horse who was very wise.

'What is REAL?' asked the Rabbit one day.

'Real… is a thing that happens to you when a child loves you for a long, long, time,' answered the Skin Horse who was always truthful. He said that sometimes it hurt being real – and that it doesn't always happen to people who break easily or have sharp edges or who have to be kept carefully.

'By the time you are REAL most of your hair has been loved off and your eyes drop out and you get loose in the joints and very shabby. But these things don't matter at all, because once you are REAL you can't be ugly – except to people who don't understand.'

I know some people who are like superior, mechanical toys, all sharp edges – but then I am grateful for all the many people I know, worn and threadbare, but very definitely REAL.

Wishing you every success with this venture.

Yours sincerely

Pat Donlon

OLWEN FOUÉRÉ

Dear Marie

Here is my contribution to the book.

It is from T.S Eliot's Four Quartets:

> We only live, only suspire
> Consumed by either fire or fire.

Spiritual sustenance arrives in many forms but, as far as words go, these usually work for me. They give me the courage to create and to risk losing all in that fiery embrace, which I do not believe can be separated from life or love.

Another favourite, particularly while I'm rehearsing for a play, is this quote from the great Samuel Beckett (who probably makes me laugh more than anyone else in the world could):

> No matter... Try again... Fail again... Fail better...

I probably don't have the punctuation right and perhaps he wouldn't have approved but that's how I hear it in my head.

With best wishes

Olwen Fouéré

MEDBH McGUCKIAN

Dear Marie

I was sent this hand-written account by an American friend when we were compiling an anthology of Irish woman poets. Its simplicity and open-heartedness flooded me like the statements of Simone Weil. The strangeness of a Belfast woman poet describing her innermost private religious experience so clearly and confidently was indeed a food that nourished someone always ravenous and starved. Someone shaky and nervous and of the 'hand in the side' persuasion! The conviction of Christ's presence in the prose is mellowed in the passionate tribute to the Virgin in the poem. I had thought Emily Lawless the more mystic until I read this. Perhaps the impact was increased by the unusual sight of the person's handwriting, the transient and yet firm quality of that, as if it were a direct message of support. One rarely finds a consciousness laying itself so entirely on the line in the matter of miracles, and yet how many times have we been helped and relieved and physically comforted in exactly the same way, and denied, like Peter, afterwards that the process was, however blind we wished ourselves, divine.

The text was found by Anne Coleman Donnelly, California.

Emily Orr was the daughter of a Methodist minister and graduated at the Royal University of Ireland with an honours degree in history, jurisdiction and political economy. She entered the Wesley Deaconess order at Ilkley in Yorkshire. She died in 1919.

Thank you for asking me to share in this.

Medbh

In my spiritual history there are certain direct and very sacred spiritual experiences which to me, at all events, have been precious confirmations of my own faith. I do not hope to convey to any other a sense of the convincing character of these experiences as they came home to me; I have long been in doubt as to whether I ought to commit them to paper, and I do so now – God knows! – only because my poor testimony may conceivably be of use to some other human soul.

Several years ago, partly under the influence of various mystical writers who have been as springs of water to my soul, – Molinos, Thomas à Kempis, Saint Teresa, and many others – partly, I believe, because of some grace of spiritual growth vouchsafed to me by God – I began to push out from the familiar paths of that un-walled garden of my soul, and to seek further adventures in the wide upland spaces where 'God's greatness flows around our incompleteness.' I began to learn more than ever before, of the mystical power and possibilities of prayer. Would that I had not so often wearied in the well-doing!

During the years of childhood and most of the years of youth my soul had dwelt solely with more or less contentment in the Methodist garden of its birth, and never till 'mind and memory flee,' can the sweetness of that first garden of the soul be forgotten or cease to flow into my heart. The first years of instruction in and practice of what some would think a very narrow form of faith, contain for me memories of ineradicable sweetness – I must again use the word – and charm. As a very young child I began to feel intensely the call of the beautiful in religion. An avenue of white roses which led to our chapel, – the coloured glass in the windows, – the cadence of an evening hymn sung when the faces of the worshippers were getting dim, – all called out feelings which I knew to be new and strangely sacred. It is strange that although a very strong current of my soul set towards ritual and stately methods in religion, so that the private use of the Book of Common Prayer was another door opened into heaven, yet nevertheless the strongest and most fragrant religious influence, apart from the personal, came to me during those years of childhood from a very quaint and stereotyped little class meeting.

Every week during the ages of 11 to 13, I was taken, child as I was, to a little class meeting, attended by grown-up and elderly women, and conducted by an old leader whose snow-white hairs made him seem to me patriarchal indeed. From the present-day point of view no means of grace could possibly have seemed more unsuitably chosen as a means of appeal to a little child, and part of its success no doubt arose from the fact that I was not conscious of there being any

definite intention of appeal. At first, 'going with mother to
class' was merely a habit in which I acquiesced, and which
soon proved itself to have strange and unexpected
opportunities of spiritual light and charm. We met in the
summer dusk or in the winter fire-light in the parlour at the
back of a little shop, the grave women filed in, took their
accustomed places with hushed greetings, and exactly the
same routine was followed from week to week. We seldom
strayed beyond a few familiar hymns, and the same ritual, as
it may be called, was used in the phrases of the leader, and
the members. And, yet, at times, in spite of the inevitable
weariness that came to the child member, there grew up in
her mind an abiding sense, never to be blotted out, of the
romance and charm of the Early Methodism, of which such a
meeting as this was the direct offshoot. These garden paths
were, perhaps, stiff and formal, but they were indeed odorous
with the scent of pure and simple living and humble
communion with God.

A beautiful garden, it is true, but still a garden! I have often
thanked God that in my case it was unrivalled, and that, as I
have said, I was able, after some years, to seek farther
adventures in surrounding spaces. I found, as thousands have
found, that the new territory is limitless land, – a land of far-
stretching distances, and of wondrous adventures. It contains
beauty and dearth; lonely and dreary byways; banks where
wild thyme grows, and where arbours break into floods of
roses. These are exotic smells as of camphire, cinnamon, and
frankincense. One passes strange wayside shrines, and
becomes acquainted with very familiar fellow-pilgrims; one's
travelling companion may one moment be a nun with her
rosary, at another, a woman wearing the quaint cap and
borders of an Early Methodist.

Here I am too sadly conscious that I can only speak as one
who has touched only the very fringe of these great matters,
and I speak of them now only in the hope that if so rich a
reward waits upon a mere beginner, some other soul may be
encouraged to press farther in…

To talk with God! How marvellous is the moment when the
soul feels that another voice has broken in, so to speak, upon

the prayer soliloquy, and one listens as to a human friend! There is no audible sound, but there seems to be the address, sometimes directly by name, and then the conversation, as it may be called, flows on quietly, uninterruptedly, with question and answer, argument and reply, as in human intercourse.

Very precious are these moments, and it is perhaps not wonderful that they come, to me, at all events, chiefly in times of crisis and sorrow! Surely they are foretastes of the uninterrupted converse to be held hereafter between the soul and the Saviour! Here direct and wonderful guidance is often given, faith is stirred up and courage is poured into the fainting soul.

For there is another stage about which I have little right to speak, but of which I yet know something – the prayer – as the mystics called it, of Absolute Quiet. To obtain that experience, one needs – at least I have needed – time, quiet, a definite preparation of mind, and passing through what may be called *stages* of prayer, or vestibules before the inner shrine has been reached. I have attained it, I believe, in the stillness of a Friends' meeting, but as a rule it is a treasure found in solitude. Of the great experiences which the mystics have found in this region of absolute interior quiet, I do not venture to speak; I only wish to add my poor testimony that I, groping as it were, on the very fringe of these mysteries, have discovered for myself that they are true. There is a moment when the soul passes beyond set forms of prayer, and then beyond that precious experience of converse with the Divine Voice into a region where 'sense grows dim and flesh retires', where one's own personal identity recedes, as it were, a pinpoint, and where the soul is conscious of God alone – God filling the spaces of the universe. God present above, below and around the meanest of his creatures, and yet not crushing, but marvellous to relate, supporting, protecting, as in the warmth of a mother's breast. There is the infinite distance, but it is the distance between child and mother.

To lose all personal consciousness, and to become merged absolutely in the consciousness of God, which is brought in such a moment as this, has been, of course, the supreme aim of many seekers in prayer, and no-one who has once felt it, can escape the memory of its power and illumination, and yet I must confess that it has seemed to me that the Hand of God has often gently turned me back from deliberately seeking the frequent repetition of such moments. Whether I have been right or wrong I do not know. These times remain in my memory as a precious treasure but some inward voice of late years seemed to warn me against the deliberate use of means which would induce this experience in prayer. No doubt I was not worthy. I have been shown that such marvels exist, but had I looked too often upon that treasure-store, it may be that my eyes would have been dazzled, and made less useful for the tasks of life.

Gradually my thought came to be as that of King Arthur, who says he 'may not wander from the allotted field before his work be done; but, being done, let visions of the night or of the day come, as they will; and many a time they come.'

There are other matters in close connection with these spiritual experiences which I only reveal, as I have said, because of possible help to some other soul. We are all aware of more or less direct revelations of Our Lord which come to us in prayer, in His House, in the warmth of sacred music, in the sweet voices of nature – in a thousand ways. For all these methods of revelation I thank Him; He has spoken to me in all; but standing out sharply and clearly in my memory, are some half dozen very notable moments, when I can only say that I was conscious of the actual Living Presence of Our Lord, in a manner never felt by me at any other time – a presence which was as real as that of a human friend. To me these moments are bulwarks of my own faith; I cannot doubt the reality of The One who thus revealed Himself to me. The experiences seemed to grow in vividness and intimacy. The first time, as far as I can remember, when I had such a new consciousness, was during an afternoon of particularly dreary district visiting. I was in one of the most wretched streets of a wretched city slum: I had reached the end of the squalid, dirty line of houses and I was physically and mentally tired. I remember looking up in weariness towards the opening of the street, where the afternoon sun was sloping to the west, when I suddenly became aware – there is no other word for it

– that Christ himself was at my side, walking with me along that dirty street. I felt Him. I knew He was there, as distinctly as if I had seen him and in that consciousness I went on gladly with my work.

On this first occasion I was not conscious of any visible presence. Some years later, we were concluding the service in our afternoon Sunday school, we had had a noisy and discouraging session; the children had been very naughty and I stood up to sing the last hymn without any feeling but that of weariness, and of relief that the duty was nearly over; when, as I sang, suddenly there grew up before my mental vision, with most startling clearness, the picture of a mighty seated Figure, majestic, tender, all-powerful. He was seated, it seemed to me, at the top of the room, looking down upon our school. In another, the form would have seemed gigantic and abnormal; here there was a brief glimpse of a marvellous Power loving and controlling all things from the lowest to the highest.

In some ways the most vivid and precious of these revelations was the following.

On one occasion I was in deep trouble and anxiety of mind: I had spent much time in thought and prayer, and my heart was full of grief over my own perplexities. One Sunday evening, after a day of conflict, I went like John Wesley, 'very unwillingly', to the evening service. I was kneeling near the door of the pew and during a long prayer I happened to look up. Then, for one brief moment, the most precious of my life, I looked into the face of Christ, 'whom I have seen for myself, and mine eyes have beheld, and not another's'. He was standing in the aisle at my left side, and the impression I got was that he had been proceeding up the aisle, and had stopped and had turned towards me as I knelt. Every detail was clear; I remember even the colour of the robe, dark green. For a moment I knelt looking into his face. I can see it now – the infinite tenderness and the infinite sorrow which seemed to have its home in his eyes. As I looked into those eyes and saw the heartbreak there, my whole nature went out to him in one awe-stricken murmur: 'Oh, sorrowful Lord! Oh sorrowful Lord!' A few weeks later war was declared…

EMILY ORR (d.1919)

The Witless Mother

I was always a poor, overworked thing,
I never was over wise;
All that I knew of heaven
I saw in my baby's eyes.

'Why didn't I look to him better?'
That's what the neighbours said;
But all the teachin' an' help I got
Came after the child was dead.

For I hadn't the sense to rear him,
I was always doin' wrong,
An' givin' my lamb such food an' drink
As could never make him strong.

He'd draw back his head from my bosom,
An' look in my face an' cry
An' I'd think what a witless mother he'd got
Till I wished that we both could die.

They said it was ignorance killed him
An' then they were sorry they spoke,
An' an ould woman bid them: 'Whisht yer chat,
For the wits o' the crathur is broke!'

But if it was bad to lose him
'Twas worse to have him back.
I was no good for nursin' the living babe –
With the dead I learned the knack.

For Rory still lay in my bosom,
He never left my arm,
An' his little clay-cold body
I could neither feed nor warm.

He'd draw back his head from my shoulder,
An' look in my face an' cry;
An' never a tear could I shed for him –
My eyes were that hot an' dry.

An' at last I thought I'd end it,
For his cries was drivin' me wild –
An' throw myself into the river
An' hide away from my child.

I was thinkin' such thoughts one evenin'
When the house was empty an' still
When all of a sudden I heard a step
On the broken ould door sill

An' I rose an' made a curtsey –
I was glad I had swept the floor –
For a great, tall Lady was standin'
On the other side o' the door.

'Twas she had the gentle footfall
An' glance that would look you through,
An' her eyes an' her skirts an' the shawl on her head
Were as blue as the sky's own blue.

She sat by my side on the settle
An' said she had time to wait,
An' she smiled that tender an' wistful
On Rory an' poor dull Kate.

Then she held out her arms for my baby,
An' laid him close to her breast;
An' he cuddled his head against her
Like a wee bird in its nest.

An' all the cryin' was over,
An' all the frettin' done:
An' I sat in quiet an' listened
To the songs the Lady sung.

Her voice was like far away music
Or the sweet, wild call of a bird,
But the songs with their queer soundin' language
Were like nothin' ever you heard.

An' when I made bold to ask her
What might be the meanin' o' them,
She said they were just old lullabies
That she'd sung in Bethlehem

An' then when the stars came peepin'
An' the night was cold an' grey,
She rose up with Rory in her arms
An' said she'd go on her way.

Her voice grew deep an' solemn
Like organ notes it rolled;
'Your child and I will journey to-night
To the gates of the City of Gold

So cease your cryin' an' frettin'
Your part in him is done,
An' the lamb that wept an' suffered here
Shall rest in the arms of My Son.'

She lifted her eyes to the golden stars
As she turned away from my door.
Maybe they made a path for the feet
That had stood on the earthen floor.

EMILY ORR (d.1919)

'Flying... is like visiting a chapel of stillness and forgiveness... For just that brief while your life has been a prayer.'

Ciaran Carty

'To talk with God! How marvellous is the moment when the soul feels that another Voice has broken in, so to speak, upon the prayer soliloquy, and one listens as to a human friend!'

Emily Orr, quoted by Medbh McGuckian

'Abandoning the orthodoxies meant and still means going on a personal journey.'

Martin Drury

'Prayer to a great extent is the expression of good wishes, loving kindness and agreeable intent towards another person.'

Kathleen Watkins

'Some days, although we cannot pray, a
prayer/utters itself.'

Carol Ann Duffy, quoted by Mary O'Donnell

'Over the years, poetry had been the most common
source of illumination and stillness for me.'

Ailbhe Smyth

'I would not turn to poetry or popes for solace or
enlightenment. I would go to Bach or Beethoven
(at times) or Schubert.'

Ian Fox

'A sense of beauty, although mutilated, distorted
and soiled remains rooted in the heart of man as
a powerful incentive.'

Simone Weil, quoted by John F Deane

DAVID MARCUS

Dear Marie

For me the greatest spiritual sustenance has always been provided by music, particularly almost anything by Beethoven, Mozart or Schubert.

Wishing your project every success.

Sincerely

David Marcus

BERTIE AHERN

During the preparations for the celebrations of the 1798 bicentenary, I happened across a powerful poem by Seamus Heaney entitled 'Requiem for the Croppies' in the Oxford Book of Ireland, *and its rhythms, sensibilities and hopeful starkness stayed with me all along the way.*

During the tense negotiations which led to the Good Friday Peace Agreement, the turmoil, tears and terror of this and former generations were all brimming in our consciousness as we tried to make 'hope and history rhyme'.

Between the swishing power of the first line of the poem – 'The pockets of our greatcoats full of barley' – and the fierce hope and certainty of the last – 'And in August the barley grew up out of the grave' – we have the hectic history of the United Irishmen who set out to create a country of equity and equality for all – Catholics, Protestants and Dissenters.

Now in this generation we have the historic opportunity to harvest the barley of peace and make of it a round cake of common endeavour and mutual respect, which will feed the deep hunger of people North and South at last.

And so I pray.

Bertie Ahern TD
Taoiseach

Requiem for the Croppies

The pockets of our greatcoats fully of barley –
No kitchens on the run, no striking camp –
We moved quick and sudden in our own country.
The priest lay behind ditches with the tramp.
A people, hardly marching – on the hike –
We found new tactics happening each day:
We'd cut through reins and rider with the pike
And stampede cattle into infantry,
Then retreat through hedges where cavalry must be thrown.

Until, on Vinegar Hill, the fatal conclave.
Terraced thousands died, shaking scythes at cannon.
The hillside blushed, soaked in our broken wave.
They buried us without shroud or coffin
And in August the barley grew up out of the grave.

SEAMUS HEANEY (1939–)

JOHN F DEANE

Dear Marie

Thanks for taking the risk… I enclose a piece that includes a poem of the same title. I hope that this will meet your requirements.

Sincere regards

John F Deane

The Fullness of Desire

I believe in God, self-broken and incomplete. I believe, after Simone Weil, in the creative impulse that was an impulse of love. That shattered His eternal self-sufficiency for the sake of the love of creatures. And He created man and all the universe broken and incomplete. In His own image. Needing to fill out that gap between God and God with the same generosity of love. Hence the ongoing travail of the earth. And we are born in a state of sin because we are not God, because we carry within us the cancer of our own self-will; we put forth the blood-red sore of the ego-flower. After the measured ballet of reason we walk slowly on the ice of mystery, because it is only mystery that can take us through the intense unbreachable wall on the other side of which we too, if we can measure that same impulse of love, can destroy our ego and let God's love take us over completely.

Simone Weil: 'We feel ourselves to be outsiders, uprooted, in exile here below. We are like Ulysses who had been carried away during his sleep by sailors and woke in a strange land, longing for Ithaca with a longing that rent his soul. Suddenly Athena opened his eyes and he saw that he was in Ithaca. In the same way every man who longs indefatigably for his country, who is distracted from his desire neither by Calypso nor by the Sirens, will one day suddenly find that he is there.'

It is a question of putting aside everything that inflates the ego. It is a question of becoming again what we were in childhood: innocent as the heron, cruel as the shark, determined as a tree at the forest's edge. To put away from us all that has made us individually self-centred and oblivious of that creating impulse of God. Human reason. Human will. Human greed. The grace of God's caring, according to Simone Weil, falls frequent as raindrops on the world, and the prospects for negativity – for 'sin'– for yielding to the downward drag of gravity – are everywhere under our feet as clay is everywhere under our feet, however we may protect ourselves from it.

When the priest breaks the host at Mass what I hear is the small breast-bone of a wren snapping in two.

Simone Weil: 'Every time that a man rises to a degree of excellence, which by participation makes of him a divine being, we are aware of something impersonal and anonymous about him. His voice is enveloped in silence. This is evident in all the great works of art or thought, in the great deeds of saints and in their words.'

Affliction, love, supreme attention, death: these are some of the things that force the ego away from itself, and the ultimate power of self-destruction is love. Human love is the most beautiful force in a beautiful world, and the most demanding; affliction, the necessary force of nature in its brute ongoing impulse of destruction leading to growth leading to death, is the most terrifying. But it is, according to Weil, and I believe her, in yielding to that ongoing movement of the world and its forces (which are, of course, the outreaches of the original impulse of the creator's love) that man and all of creation will find itself at home again. Affliction, that imposed by the necessities of nature and not by the omnipresent ego-claims of men, forces us into an awareness of our mortality, of our true state here on earth.

Simone Weil: 'People often reproach Christianity for a morbid preoccupation with suffering and grief. This is an error. Christianity is not concerned with suffering and grief, for they are sensations, psychological states, in which a perverse indulgence is always possible; its concern is with something quite different, which is affliction. Affliction is not a psychological state; it is a pulverization of the soul by the mechanical brutality of circumstances. The transformation of

a man, in his own eyes, from the human condition into that of
a half-crushed worm writhing on the ground is a process
which not even a pervert would find attractive. Neither does
it attract a sage, a hero, or a saint. Affliction is something
which imposes itself upon a man quite against his will. Its
essence, the thing it is defined by, is the horror, the revulsion
of the whole being, which it inspires in its victim. And this is
the very thing one must consent to, by virtue of supernatural
love.'

I have been given a Christian name but have not earned the
right to be called Christian.

But one of the ways in which – *pace* the seeming contradiction
– I have found myself able to pass away out of the demands
of the ego is in the total attention to a poem, and to writing
poems. To allow the experiences I have lived through to settle
and to send forth some sign that they have found a
meaningful settling-place is to attend, totally and for however
short and intense a period, to the demands of language, of
movement, sound, and meaning, to put the self away and let
the experience speak out of its own depth.

Simone Weil: 'A sense of beauty, although mutilated,
distorted, and soiled, remains rooted in the heart of man as a
powerful incentive. It is present in all the preoccupations of
secular life. If it were made true and pure, it would sweep all
secular life in a body to the feet of God; it would make the
total incarnation of the faith possible... Art is an attempt to
transport into a limited quantity of matter, modelled by man,
an image of the infinite beauty of the entire universe. If the
attempt succeeds, this portion of matter should not hide the
universe, but on the contrary it should reveal its reality to all
around.'

After the agitated moments, the search for calm; and the
uncompromising, deeply felt and clearly reasoned thoughts
of Simone Weil, particularly in the collection *Gravity and
Grace*, I have found will lead me to a reflective calm that does,
at times (for even our strongest powers flop and flag so often
under the pressures of our ego-carapaces), overcome the
slings and arrows ...

The Fullness of Desire

Mist in the forenoon, cattle shifting
languorously, their wet eyes watching;
over the fields hung Good Friday mystery;

we stood about, waiting; a hare, big bucko,
sat attentive; surviving buckshot, his kind
has grown fluid in the arts of living.

We had gathered after a death; big men,
naturally sure among the animals, shifted
awkward with suits, awkward with belief;

the coffin had been received, he will go down
wearing a fine blood-rose in his lapel.
They have gone home now, honey-lights on the altar

have been quenched; do you remember –
in the age of innocence – the stations? how we went
round slowly in the lugubrious dance, the

Stabat mater, the *flectamus genua*; how we knew
we had generosity and love to lift us
somewhere between earth and heaven?

The altar has been stripped for the ceremony;
the rest of the day will be coloured purple;
I kneel in a dim cave of silence; the man,

moved to a side aisle, has found repose;
there is the soft creak of benches, pale light
palely filtered, the hidden sun will set early;

nothing miraculous to be expected; what is demanded
is the obedience of stillness, the slaking of thirst
with bitterness, the prolonged suffering that is love.

Attend. Be faithful. Grow fluid. Be at peace.

JOHN F DEANE (1943–)

MAUREEN POTTER

The meaning of the last part of life is expressed in a poem by Jenny Joseph. This poem has been a favourite of mine for years. Even before the BBC discovered it.

I'm not sure it gives me spiritual sustenance but I love its spirited independence and individuality. I hope to follow her lead and trust that when I don the purple it will not cause tremors in the diocese or consternation in the consistory.

Maureen Potter

Warning

When I am an old woman I shall wear purple
With a red hat which doesn't go, and doesn't suit me
And I shall spend my pension on brandy and summer gloves
And satin sandals, and say we've no money for butter.
I shall sit down on the pavement when I'm tired
And gobble up samples in shops and press alarm bells
And run my stick along the public railings
And make up for the sobriety of my youth.
I shall go out in my slippers in the rain
And pick the flowers in other people's gardens
And learn to spit.

You can wear terrible shirts and grow more fat
And eat three pounds of sausages at a go
Or only bread and pickle for a week
And hoard pens and pencils and beermats and things in boxes.

And now we must have clothes that keep us dry.
And pay rent and not swear in the street
And set a good example for the children
We must have friends to dinner and read the papers.

But maybe I ought to practise a little now?
So people who know me are not too shocked and surprised
When suddenly I am old and start to wear purple.

JENNY JOSEPH (1932–)

DONALD CAIRD

But the souls of the righteous are in the hands of God and no torment shall ever touch them. In the eyes of the foolish they seem to have died, and their departure was thought to be an affliction, and their going from us to be their destruction; but they are at peace.

For though in the sight of men they were punished, their hope is full of immortality. Having been disciplined a little, they will receive great good because God tested them and found them worthy of himself; like gold in the fire he tried them, and like a sacrificial burnt offering he accepted them.

In the time of their visitation they will shine forth and will run like sparks through stubble. They will govern nations and rule over peoples and the Lord will reign over them forever. Those who trust in Him will understand truth, and the faithful will abide with him in love, because grace and mercy are upon his elect and he watches over his holy ones.

THE WISDOM OF SOLOMON 3: 1-9

Dear Editor

This is a magnificent pre-Christian expression of belief in a life after death, not as an inherent right or quality of human nature, but as a gift of God, a God who is righteous and merciful.

It stands in elegant contrast to the common and perhaps prevailing belief in Western society that death ends everything, dissolving all relationships, wiping out all responsibilities, rendering all value judgements of right and wrong meaningless and superfluous, when a purely physical system, the human body, returns to the physical elements of which it was composed, one hundred and fifty pounds of albumenoid matter, dissolves without remainder into its physical components, leaving nothing.

Immanuel Kant saw the utter bankruptcy of such a philosophy, concluding that a life after death in a moral environment is a necessary postulate of practical (moral) reason.

We cannot think cogently in terms of right and wrong without postulating a life after death according to Kant, however much the experience of our senses may militate against it .

This beautiful Hebrew writing makes it easier to believe.

✠ The Most Revd Dr Donald Caird
(Former Archbishop of Dublin)

ROGER STALLEY

On July 8th 1933 an American scholar, by the name of Arthur Kingsley Porter, was lost off the coast of Inisbofin (Donegal) in rather mysterious circumstances. Porter was a professor at Harvard and an expert on the architecture and sculpture of the middle ages. After his death, his widow explained how he first came to study medieval art. Taking time off as a student of law, he was visiting the Gothic cathedral of Coutances in Normandy, when the sun broke through the traceried windows, illuminating the architecture in a manner that he could never forget. He knew then that he could not become a lawyer. I suspect that most people who admire medieval art have had similar, though perhaps not quite as decisive, experiences as that which affected Kingsley Porter at Coutances.

It was the aim of Gothic builders to reproduce on earth monuments which gave a hint of celestial glories, and how well they succeeded. In many cases relentless tourism has broken the spell, but in the winter months, one can sit in almost total solitude in Chartres Cathedral, absorbing the vastness of the space, charged with a kaleidoscope of colour: at Chartres there are one hundred and eighteen medieval windows filling the cathedral with shafts of saturated light. A transcendental experience was exactly what the thirteenth-century builders sought to achieve and it is still there to be enjoyed today.

It is not just the aesthetic effect that makes this a moving experience, but the fact that it was created over seven hundred and fifty years ago. In such circumstances it is hard not to contemplate the unfolding of history and the passage of time. At Chartres this very point is made in the sculptures of the Royal Portal, where the arches are carved with the signs of the zodiac and the appropriate rural labour for each month of the year, a spiritual time clock on the walls of the cathedral. And then there is the sheer quality of the craftsmanship. In some windows this has added poignancy, for there are depictions of donors – vintners, furriers, sculptors, and other tradesmen of Chartres – advertising their profession like twentieth-century sponsors.

Of course there are plenty of other Gothic buildings which offer equivalent experiences, the cathedrals at Bourges, for example, or even the church of St Pierre, down in the town of Chartres, which remains unknown to most travellers.

What makes these monuments so special is a cocktail of spiritual feelings, a combination of fine architecture, light, history and distance. The fact that the monuments are situated abroad adds another crucial ingredient, for it means they are normally explored on occasions when the routines of life have been temporarily suspended; herein lies one of the fundamental differences in the appreciation of art and literature. The best of modern photography can never convey the feeling of actually being there. In art and architecture experiences tend to be transitory: one looks, knowing that the opportunity is unlikely to be repeated. We are getting a glimpse of something we can never make our own.

Irish medieval monuments do not reach the sublime levels of Bourges or Chartres. But there are plenty of lonely abbeys, where the combination of silence, landscape and wrought stone evokes similar emotions. For me there are places like Athassel, a huge Augustinian abbey situated beside the river Suir in County Tipperary or the sculptured crosses in the old graveyard at Ahenny. But it is hard to beat Corcomroe, enveloped by the mountains of the Burren, which Betjeman seemed to record so well:

In Ireland with Emily

Stony seaboard, far and foreign,
Stony hills poured over space,
Stony outcrop of the Burren,
Stones in every fertile place...
Till there rose abrupt and lonely,
A ruined abbey, chancel only,
Lichen-crusted, time befriended,
Soared the arches splayed and splendid,
Romanesque against the sky.

JOHN BETJEMAN (1906–84)

For years I was convinced that these words were written about Corcomroe, but the personal papers of the poet apparently indicate that it was the old church at Drumacoo which he had in mind. I remain sceptical, for Drumacoo is some distance from the stony hills of the Burren. But what do Corcomroe and countless similar monuments offer in the way of spiritual sustenance? For a start there is a sense of wonder at the finesse of the ancient craftsmen, who managed to cut the tough intractable stone; there is also the sense of humour that monks and masons seemed to share, revealed in the masonry dragon that crawls down the corners of the chancel; there is the harmony between the stone of the abbey and the surrounding landscape; and there is the silence, broken only by the birds and the sounds of distant tractors. In fact some of the emotions we feel today are exactly those which moved the early monks. When Ailred of Rievaulx tried to explain the rewards of the monastic life, he did so with the comment: 'Everywhere peace, everywhere serenity, and a marvellous freedom from the tumult of the world.' These words (or at least the Latin equivalent of them) were written in the twelfth century.

Roger Stalley

ALICE TAYLOR

The Quiet Face

It was an evening in mid February. The sunset was a soft
yellow glow washed through with waves of misty blue. The
sea and the sky melted together and the sun ran a yellow
stream between them.

I sat on a rock on the water's edge but my mind floated
between the sea and the sky. The sun slowly sank and sent
rays of peace into my heart.

But there was more joy to come when the sky became a pink
lady of many shades admiring her reflection in the sea. She
spread her floating cloak along the horizon and only when
darkness crept over her shoulder did she finally melt into the
water. She took my problems and tensions with her. I came
home at peace with myself and the world.

So many times during my life the sunset has done great
things for me. I live beside a river and woods and they are
wonderful in themselves but the sunset dresses them in
exquisite colours. Maybe the sunset is the face of God.

Alice Taylor

IMOGEN STUART

Dear Marie Heaney

Thank you for asking me to send you words which mean something special to me. I am very pleased and honoured to be included in your publication. The choice was terribly hard for me. I have a little book into which I write poems and sayings that mean a lot to me. I read them quite often: poems that I love. I also use them to comfort grieving friends. This time I selected sayings which are related to my work as a sculptor. I had to cut them down ruthlessly to six, to the most important ones which will be meaningful to everybody. They were all written by wonderful people!

I would be most grateful if you could squeeze them all in.

Greetings and kind regards

Imogen Stuart

By being the curator of our images we care for our souls.

THOMAS MOORE

Taste, touch and smell, hearing and seeing are not only or merely a means to sensation, enjoyable or otherwise, but they are also a means to knowledge and are indeed our only actual means to knowledge.

ERIC GILL

The senses are a kind of reason.

ST THOMAS AQUINAS

Kurosaw, more than any other artist, has fulfilled his own bidding: 'Each artist must create his own universe.'

The rococo style has a place in civilisation. Serious-minded people may call it shallow and corrupt; well, the founders of the American constitution, who were far from frivolous, thought fit to mention the pursuit of happiness as a proper aim for mankind, and if ever this aim has been given visible form it is in rococo architecture – the pursuit of happiness and the pursuit of love.

KENNETH CLARKE

The architect Leon Battista Alberti addressed man in these words: 'To you is given a body more graceful than other animals, to you the power of apt and various movements, to you most sharp and delicate senses, to you wit, reason, memory like an immortal god'.

KENNETH CLARKE

BRIAN FARRELL

Dear Marie

The very thought of dredging up readings that give spiritual sustenance is daunting. I'm not sure that, at this phase of my life, I have anything at all to offer that would fit even within the parameters of a generous interpretation of the term 'spiritual sustenance'. Maybe you might consider some of my favourite 'comfort readings'?

Certainly when I was younger – a rather serious and somewhat solitary adolescent – I was drawn to Chesterton and Belloc and through them to Francis Thompson. It was, in the narrow sense of the term, a quite Catholic range. It was also romantic. There is still something attractive in the innocence of GKC's 'The Queen of Seven Swords' – and, despite the consciously 'poetic' style and idiom, considerable technical capacity in carrying both theme and structure through the seven poems given to the great patrons of Christendom. 'St Patrick of Ireland' offers a good example and springs straight from memory.

> Mine eyes were alive with anger;
>   for the gag was in my mouth.
> They bound me to a broken tree,
>   with my face towards the South
> And hucksters watched and betted,
>   when would the great heart break
> And pygmy pedants whipped me,
>   for Thy name's sake

As for Thompson's 'Hound of Heaven', I still fancy that the emphatic rhythm and ready rhyme, as much as the tortuous imagery, self-absorption and inflated language might bring solace to some of today's teenagers.

> I fled Him, down the nights and down the days;
> I fled Him, down the arches of the years;
> I fled Him, down the labyrinthine ways
> Of my own mind; and in the mist of tears
> I hid from Him, and under running laughter,

Up vistaed hopes I sped;
And shot, precipitated,
Adown Titanic glooms of chasmed fears,
From those strong Feet that followed, followed after.
But with unhurrying chase,
And unperturbed pace,
Deliberate speed, majestic instancy,
They beat – and a Voice beat
More instant than the Feet –
'All things betray thee, who betrayest Me.'

Later, as a clerical student, an excellent teacher tried to persuade me to a more intellectual, muscular kind of spiritual reading. Newman, in particular, was recommended; I duly, and dutifully, ploughed through his Apologia. But, truth to tell, I wasn't able to find much spiritual sustenance there. I would still prefer the memory of those poets I discovered for myself when I was young.

Much later again, I was more inclined to look to other old favourites; not so much for spiritual sustenance as for comfort. Typically in the post-flu convalescent phase I would drop whatever thriller was failing to raise my spirits and make for David Copperfield. *It's a book that retains its magic for a range of reasons. Partly because it was one of the first substantial novels I found for myself. A big, solid read for a little boy for ever short of reading material in a home short on books.*

It attracted me – as Dickens still does – because his books were full of bustle and life and extraordinary people. I was also conscious that the novel was, at least in part, based on Dickens's own life experiences and saw in its development of the fortunate circumstances that brought young David from unhappy childhood to adulthood many echoes of my own life. Not least I shared with young Copperfield a disrupted childhood.

In my case it was moving from an Irish family in Manchester to becoming an evacuee and virtually an only child in Dublin. I had personal experience of a godmother, who, like Betsy Trotwood, became a saving angel transforming my life chances. Those crazy coincidences and chance encounters that Dickens used to solve problems with his plots I found entirely plausible – even, on some dark days, promises of hope.

Quite by accident I came across quite a different David's story and found a book to which I've often turned for comfort. For all the attention paid to Primo Levi and the more recent fuss about the Oscar-winning Life is Beautiful, I have always found it difficult to come to terms with the holocaust. That such a terrifying and scandalous slaughter should happen in our continent in our lifetime is a challenge to us all – and, fortunately, I think that sense of outraged challenge is evident in public response to the tragedy of Kosovo.

For a very long time I could find no piece of writing that could salvage any vestige of human hope, let alone understanding, from that terrible experience. Then one day in bed, recovering from a cold and desperately short of reading material I dug in the school-bag of one of my teenage children and discovered I am David – the story of a little boy wandering through the nightmare of World War II and, protected by innocence and good fortune, finding his mother. Of course it's sentimental and romantic but I've read it more than once as a life-enhancing allegory of one of the darkest days that Europe has known. For many years it was stuffed in a locker beside my bed but when I just now went looking, it – like so many other books – has gone missing.

What do I read now for comfort? Often enough it's a matter of returning to old favourites. In particular there are a few poems that recapture memories and rattle the bars of contemporary life; poems I return to not only because they are full of golden moments of my past but also because they have within them new resonances that cast light on the present.

Fixed, like a key-stone in the arch of memory, a Saturday morning in the old UCD building in Earlsfort Terrace in 1950. I was attending a freshman English tutorial by Roger McHugh. He was bursting with his own enthusiasm, guiding us with a contrived casualness to some appreciation of what poetry has to say. Coming to the end of the class he opened his Collected Poems of Yeats and said 'Listen to this,' as he recited:

Memory

One had a lovely face,
And two or three had charm,
But charm and face were in vain
Because the mountain grass
Cannot but keep the form
Where the mountain hare has lain

WB YEATS (1865–1939)

It's a poem that says so much, with such deceptive simplicity, about human experience and those great virtues of loyalty and endurance. It is at once immediate in its emotional intensity and profoundly deep in its implications. And it reminds me of a rich, fulfilling, exciting time in my life.

So, too, does Seamus Heaney's 'Villanelle for an Anniversary', a formal poem, written to commemorate Harvard's 350th anniversary celebration in 1986. To come from the still grey post-war deprivation of Dublin to the riches of the Widener Library, from a still small and confined UCD to a great university, all of this was a kind of miracle. But I was also conscious that Harvard's own beginnings had been modest.

In this poem Heaney at once captures the simplicity – even the remoteness – of that time and the underlying promise of what was to come. It's a poem full of hope, history and aspiration; it's also carefully and cleverly constructed with its repetitions to carry across the vast crowd gathered around Harvard Square for the festive occasion. But, most of all, for me it's a poem full of artifice and energy that reminds me of one of the happiest and most fulfilling times in my life – truly, I think, a work of spiritual sustenance. I first read it in an American journal and was immediately brought back to my own miraculously exciting year in Cambridge, Mass., as a graduate student in the mid-1950s. Now, happily, it's available in Opened Ground: Poems 1966-1996.

Sincerely
Brian Farrell

Villanelle for an Anniversary

A spirit moved, John Harvard walked the yard,
The atom lay unsplit, the west unwon,
The books stood open and the gates unbarred.

The maps dreamt on like moondust. Nothing stirred.
The future was a verb in hibernation.
A spirit moved, John Harvard walked the yard.

Before the classic style, before the clapboard,
All through the small hours of an origin,
The books stood open and the gates unbarred.

Night passage of a migratory bird.
Wingflap. Gownflap. Like a homing pigeon
A spirit moved, John Harvard walked the yard.

Was that his soul (look) sped to its reward
By grace or works? A shooting star? An omen?
The books stood open and the gates unbarred.

Begin again where frosts and tests were hard.
Find yourself or founder. Here, imagine
A spirit moved, John Harvard walked the yard.
The books stood open and the gates unbarred.

SEAMUS HEANEY (1939–)

JOHN MONTAGUE

Marie

'Let nothing disturb you/Nothing affright you.' I murmur these lines translated from St Theresa of Avila, when things are becoming hairy. Or if I am in a more pagan mood, the great farewell of Walter Savage Landor:

> I strove with none for none were worth my strife,
> Nature I loved and next to nature, Art:
> I warmed both hands before the fire of life;
> It sinks, and I am ready to depart.

WALTER SAVAGE LANDOR (1775–1864)

Christian, pagan, can be succeeded by Eastern or Tantric practice. It is so sustaining to love, to be loved, and to make love, although it is not a solace that would occur to King Lear raging on the heath.

So far, despite periods of sturm und drang, *I have enjoyed life, but then I have had the good luck to be talented, even if in the least lucrative of literary forms, and to be in mainly good health, with only the usual setbacks. Certain forms of mental pain, the black dog of depression (Robert Burns's 'blue devil'), I find hard to endure, but, when the clouds part, you often see something you did not see before. Extreme physical pain may also bring some kind of illumination, but I would prefer not to try the experiment. And, as for death itself... Only in India have I felt free of our Western fear of death, and sensed it as part of a greater process, a change of state, an abandoning of a worn-out physical husk, perhaps for something else.*

John Montague

DAVID KERR

Dear Marie

Thank you for the invitation to contribute to your new publication.

The text I have chosen is one of Charles Wesley's hymns. This hymn expresses a core belief of the seventy million or so Methodists throughout the world and has formed a central core of my own spirituality. As I look back over the years I can see that the sentiments expressed have shaped my own understanding of God and his relationship to people. Over the years I have often lost track of the hymn, rarely referring to it. However, in the past few years I have found myself returning to it again and again to find affirmations for the things which resonate most deeply for me as a person.

The whole hymn expresses amazement at the love of God freely offered to all people unconditionally, just as they are. This has meant much to me as I have struggled to respond to that love in my own life and to give meaning to it in relationships with other people. When I am under pressure and feel that I am being criticised and judged this hymn speaks to me of an accepting God who takes me just as I am and through his 'amazing love' seeks to recreate his own image within me.

This ongoing life-sharing experience with God through Jesus Christ has been 'a quickening ray' on the very darkest of nights of self doubt. In fact it becomes a liberating experience which enables me to walk free from past failure and mistakes in the pursuit of that love embodied in the life and death of Jesus Christ.

As I struggle to offer some small strand of leadership in the emerging Ireland, full as it is of divisions and exclusions, I find myself driven back to its central affirmation that God's love is free equally for all the people of the world. And I turn again to the task of living from this insight among the rich diversity of the peoples who inhabit this most beautiful of islands.

Yours sincerely

Rev David J Kerr
President of the Methodist Church

And can it be

And can it be that I should gain
An interest in the Saviour's blood?
Died he for me, who caused his pain?
For me, who him to death pursued?
Amazing love! How can it be
That thou, my God, shouldst die for me?

'Tis mystery all: the Immortal dies!
Who can explore his strange design?
In vain the first-born seraph tries
To sound the depths of love divine.
'Tis mercy all! Let earth adore,
Let angel minds enquire no more.

He left his Father's throne above –
So free, so infinite his grace –
Emptied himself of all but love,
And bled for Adam's helpless race.
'Tis mercy all, immense and free;
For, O my God, it found out me!

Long my imprisoned spirit lay
Fast bound in sin and nature's night;
Thine eye diffused a quickening ray –
I woke, the dungeon flamed with light,
My chains fell off, my heart was free,
I rose, went forth, and followed thee.

No condemnation now I dread;
Jesus, and all in him, is mine!
Alive in him, my living Head,
And clothed in righteousness divine,
Bold I approach the eternal throne,
And claim the crown, through Christ, my own.

CHARLES WESLEY (1707–88)

SEÁN Mac RÉAMOINN

Dear Marie

I have always admired the hard diamond-like sparkle of 'A Bhean Lán de Stuaim' – one of the last poems in the tradition of Gaelic amour courtois, which flourished from the 14th century to the 17th century. But my appreciation of it has deepened as I have come to recognise the ambiguity of the poet's reluctance to engage: was it moral principle, or had he simply reached an age where he could no longer take Yes! for an answer?

A Bhean Lán de Stuaim

A bhean lán de stuaim
coingibh uaim do lámh:
ní fear gníomha sinn,
cé taoi tinn dar ngrádh.

Féach ar liath dem fholt,
féach mo chorp gan lúth,
féach ar thraoch dem fhuil –
créad ré bhfuil do thnúth?

Ná saoil mé go saobh,
arís ná claon do cheann;
bíodh ar ngrádh gan ghníomh
go bráth, a shíodh sheang.

Druid do bhéal óm bhéal,
doiligh an scéal do chor –
ná bíom cneas re cneas:
tig ón teas an tol.

Do chúl craobhach cas,
do rosc glas mar dhrúcht,
do chíoch chruinngheal bhláith,
tharraingeas mian súl.

Gach gníomh acht gníomh cuirp
is luighe id chuilt shuain
do-ghéan féin tréd ghrádh,
a bhean lán de stauim.

<small>BRIAN MAC GIOLLA PHÁDRAIG</small> (C 1580–1652)

O Lady Full of Guile

O lady full of guile,
take away your hand.
Though you sicken for my love,
I am not an active man.

Consider my grey hairs.
Consider my slack body.
Consider my tired blood.
What is it you want?

Don't think I am perverse.
You need not tilt your head.
Let's love without the deed
for ever, spirit slender.

Take your mouth from mine:
grave is your condition.
– touch not skin to skin
the heat leads on to lust.

Your branching curly hair,
your eye as grey as dew,
your sweet pale rounded breast
excite the eye alone.

All deeds but that of the flesh
–and lying in your quilt –
I will do for love of you,
O lady full of guile.

Translated by <small>THOMAS KINSELLA</small> (1929-)

Seathrún Céitinn (15th/16th century), historian, poet (this poem has been improbably attributed to him) and priest of the Counter-Reformation, might not have recognised his contemporary, George Herbert, as a fellow-priest. But he would have relished his poetry. This poem is for all who pray, and for those of us who want to, but can't or have forgotten how.

Love
Seán

Prayer

Prayer: the church's banquet, angels' age.
    God's breath in man returning to his birth,
    The soul in paraphrase, heart in pilgrimage,
The Christian plummet sounding heaven and earth;

Engine against the Almighty, sinners' tower,
    Reversed thunder, Christ-side-piercing spear,
    The six-days' world transposing in an hour,
A kind of tune which all things hear and fear;

Softness, and peace, and joy, and love, and bliss,
    Exalted manna, gladness of the best,
    Heaven in ordinary, man well dressed,
The Milky Way, the bird of paradise,
    Church bells beyond the stars heard, the soul's blood,
    The land of spices; something understood.

GEORGE HERBERT (1593-1632)

DEREK HILL

Dear Marie Heaney

The epitaph I wrote for my own grave is:

> Peace was all I ever asked
> 'Twas all that was denied
> The Angels of the Lord
> It seemed
> Fought on the other side.

Composed in Donegal and I won a mention in a poetry competition at Ballyshannon which I collected after lunch with Lord Mountbatten the Saturday before his death. He was killed on the Monday and if it hadn't been for this poetry award collection... he wanted me to go out on his boat that same afternoon!

Emily Dickinson, probably the greatest of all American poets, wrote

> Wild Nights – Wild Nights!
> Were I with thee
> Wild Nights should be
> Our luxury!
>
> Futile – the winds –
> To a heart in port –
> Done with the Compass –
> Done with the Chart!
>
> Rowing in Eden –
> Ah, the sea!
> Might I but moor – Tonight –
> In Thee.

> EMILY DICKINSON (1830-86)

Also very inspiring. Hope this helps!

Derek Hill

MAIREAD NÍ MHAONAIGH

Dear Marie

I'm delighted to be part of this publication for such a good cause.

Ar scath a chéile a mhaireann na daoine
(Man is not alone in this world).[2]

It was during my husband Frankie Kennedy's illness and eventual death that I realised the amount of goodness there is in this world.

Love is there for all of us. All we have to do is open our hearts and accept it.

I felt hopeless and devastated by my loss but I also felt a great love surrounding and protecting me - as if I was in a secure cocoon, a cocoon of love.

I also realised and understood the term 'eternal love' for although Frankie had passed away the love between us has remained.

In Donegal, where I come from, we say 'Tá mo chroí istigh ionat' (My heart is within you), for 'I love you'.

After Frankie died I found my despair and loneliness hard to describe – words seemed inadequate and limited. Music became my solace, my expression, my prayer, my life. It reached the depths of my soul and caressed the anger, the guilt, the pain and brought a glimmer of hope and light into my life. Healing meant accepting my situation and continuing my life to the whole.

It is true to say that at the moment of death one is more alive than ever – it seems a contradiction but it is real. Truth is present: there is no time for sentimentality.

I thank God to have had the privilege of knowing Frankie and to have had the honour of helping him into the other life.

Now I know that life is good.

Give wholeheartedly, open and receive.

Is mise, le meas,

Mairead Ní Mhaonaigh

---

2 Literally: People live in one another's shadows.

Lúireach Phádraig
(St Patrick's Breastplate)

Críost liom,
Críost romham,
Críost i mo dhiaidh,
Críost i mo láimh dheis,
Críost i mo láimh chlé,
Críost fúim,
Críost os mo cheann,
Críost i mo shuí,
Críost i mo luí,
Críost i m'éirigh,
Críost i gcroí gach duine a smaoineas orm,
Críost i mbéal gach duine a labhras liom,
Críost i súil gach duine a dhearcas orm,
Críost i ngach cluas a chluineas me.

TRADITIONAL

SACHA ABERCORN

Dear Marie

Like most people, I grew up thinking the churches and the words of the clergy were the unique mediums through which the spirit expressed itself. If that were the case, however, I soon discovered that such expression did not have the answers I required in my hour of need, and conveyed no sense of what I believed spirituality to be. Such expression failed to connect, for me, with 'the heart of the matter'. It only spoke of things that were out of reach.

On the other hand, I began to discover a more profound message in such things as the struggle of a butterfly emerging from its chrysalis, or the comforting purl of a flowing river, or the haunting cry of a curlew in the marshes.

Gradually, too, as I developed an understanding of my own dream world and inner reality, I began to find a sense of the sacred in certain works of the creative imagination – certain paintings, certain pieces of music, certain works of literature – as well as in the ritual of the dance and the sound of the human voice raised in song or prayer.

I had crossed a threshold, undergone a rite of passage. I had experienced an initiation. As a result of that initiation, I believe I now have a sense, which I did not before, of the nature of spirituality.

Like the soft breath of a breeze brushing a smooth skin of water – so the spirit moves through our lives. It is something so intangible, yet so powerful; and it manifests itself, according to the moment, in so many forms.

Thus there are times when, instead of a breeze, it is like the steady flame of a candle burning gently in the darkness. At other times, it is more like a spark of brightness leaping from an immense fire, dancing here and there, enlivening everything it touches. At yet other moments, it can almost be felt as a thread to be held and followed – perhaps the red thread that Ariadne held for Theseus as he entered the labyrinth to confront the Minotaur, or the red thread of blood pursuing its course through the labyrinth of the body.

Intimations of the spirit have been captured and conveyed by all great artists from time immemorial, often in their depictions of nature and the natural world. Such intimations are also like Ariadne's thread, leading us back through the labyrinth of our collective history and teaching us, in the process, where we tended to go astray.

Prior to the Enlightenment, the so-called Age of Reason, spirit and nature were not divided from each other. The sun and the moon guided the extroversion and the introversion of our lives, as did the rhythms of organic existence around us and the cycles of the seasons. We were in tune and in contact with a higher principle, which we defied at our peril. As much as we yearned for the light, we respected the dark.

But through our yearning for the light, our striving for more consciousness, we found ourselves moving further and further up a mountain. We found ourselves moving into the rarefied and ever thinner air of the rational, the academic, the scientific, the technological – a realm where there was, supposedly, a 'reasonable' answer to everything. And in so doing, we left behind us, down in the valleys, our natural instinctual life, the world of earthy feeling, the domain of the senses.

The split between light and dark in our being – between spirit and nature – is something we all experience, to a greater or lesser extent, in our personal lives. It is visible in the schisms, divides and fissures that occur in our communities and amongst nations. And it is exacerbated by our educational system.

If there is nothing in place, no bridge to connect our fragmented realities – the reality of the head and that of the heart – a breakdown ensues. This moment of breakdown or crisis will develop in one of two ways. The rent or wound may be masked or sealed over, trapping the pain within and causing it to fester. Or the pain can be experienced and lived with until we can break through to a new level of consciousness – consciousness of the spirit, which performs its own act of healing.

This often painful renewal of ourselves through the spirit is a process that needs nurturing and sustaining.

The renewing spirit does not speak to us only from the light at the top of the mountain. It also speaks to us from the depths of the dark – from the valleys of despair.

It speaks to our whole being, to our bodies, our minds and our emotions. It is sustained by the ways we learn to relate to the totality of our natures and to those around us.

It needs the closeness of human touch, the warmth of skin against skin, and it also needs stillness and solitude – the self-contained integrity of a candle burning in the dark.

It is sustained by our hands in the earth, weeding or pulling at briars, and by recording a dream, and by unlocking the resonances of the symbolic world.

It is sustained by the cathedral-like serenity of a majestic beech wood bathed in dappled light; and it is sustained, too, by the womb-like confines of a subterranean chapel aglow with the radiance of holy icons.

It is sustained by the reconnection to the child within – as when the realm of fairy tale links us to our own life's journey and furnishes us with the magical means of surmounting our fear of the surrounding shadows. And thus we are emotionally strengthened and emboldened to confront ever-greater obstacles as we grow and mature.

The renewing spirit is sustained by the laughter, the spontaneity, the sheer fun enjoyed amongst friends and loved ones; and it is sustained, too, by the deepest sonorities of certain chords that carry us with them into the infinite.

It is sustained by the twisting, turning, serpentine pathways we experience as we walk the labyrinth to the centre of our being. And it is sustained when we bring into focus the all-important plumb line – the backbone of our being – that runs through us and unites us with both heaven and earth.

Such now is my understanding of spirituality. I find it conveyed to me by the natural world and by buildings or structures that encourage a sense of personal space and inner tranquillity. I find it conveyed by certain paintings and certain pieces of music. I find it conveyed in fairy tales, especially those my father himself composed for me during my childhood. I find it in the richness of archetypal myth and legend – the story of Psyche and Eros, for example, or of Theseus and Ariadne in the labyrinth.

The works of CG Jung, such as Memories, Dreams, Reflections, *have conveyed to me much spiritual insight and understanding. So, too, have those of his disciples – Frances Wickes, for example, in* The Inner World of Childhood. *And because of the Russian element in my own ancestry, I find spiritual sustenance in works that evoke the*

Russian soil and soul, such as Turgenev's Hunting Sketches *and Nabokov's* Speak, Memory.

Novels, too, are often a source of spiritual sustenance for me – established classics, like those of Tolstoy and Dostoyevsky, and more recent works, like The Chymical Wedding *by Lindsay Clarke. And, of course, there is poetry. Among the poems from which I've derived spiritual inspiration, I should mention 'Say Not the Struggle Nought Availeth' by Arthur Hugh Clough and, in superb new translation by the late Ted Hughes, 'The Prophet' by Alexander Pushkin. I must also mention the poems of DH Lawrence, such as 'Snake', and of WB Yeats, such as 'Into the Twilight' and 'The Man Who Dreamed of Fairyland'. And I find a particularly stirring spiritual energy in the works of Rainer Maria Rilke, from one of whose poems, 'Wendung' or 'Turning Point', I should like to quote the last stanza.*

All best wishes

Sacha

from Wendung

Work of seeing achieved,
now attempt heart-work
on all the images prisoned within; for you
dominated them but do not yet know them.
Recognise, O man within, your own inner maiden,
she who's been distilled from a thousand natures, she
who's only been distilled, but never,
as yet, beloved.

RAINER MARIA RILKE (1875–1926)

GILLIAN BOWLER

Dear Marie

I keep putting this off; I'm finding it amazingly difficult to do. Not to choose the text, but the revealing and explanation of my reasons. A confused mix of privacy, and a lack of belief in any formal religious ethos, holds me back.

But I do believe that spirituality exists in all of us, whatever our beliefs or lack of them. And I remember, even when I was very young, six or seven, learning James Elroy Flecker's 'To a Poet a Thousand Years Hence' by heart, so that I could hug it to myself, for comfort – which I still do, forty years on.

One particular text comes to mind though, which makes this task easier, requiring no words or reasons from me to help deliver or add to its message.

There is an inscription on a third-century tomb at Umm Quais, in Jordan – an Ottoman village overlooking the Sea of Galilee. It reads:

> To you I say, passer-by:
> As you are, I used to be
> And as I am, you will be.
> Use life as a mortal.

Gillian Bowler

GABRIEL FITZMAURICE

Hello Marie

Many thanks for your kind invitation to contribute to your proposed anthology and to a worthy cause. I wish you every success.

Yes! There are a number of texts that I draw sustenance from as I stumble through life. 'Dark Night of the Soul' and 'Living Flame of Love' by Saint John of the Cross immediately come to mind; the Bhagavad Gita and the Upanishads from the Hindu tradition have helped me along the way; as have the Analects of Confucius, the Tao Te Ching; there are many books on Zen Buddhism that I return to regularly; and Martin Buber's I And Thou, which my friend Pádraig Hogan bought for me the first time we visited Shakespeare and Company in Paris, is a constant source of inspiration. One of my favourite texts is the Sermon on the Mount which I chose for Lifelines 2. But the text I choose for you is a poem by Robert Frost. For the following reasons…

There's a dúchas in my family, particularly on my mother's side, towards melancholy and song. Being very much my mother's son, I'm no stranger to both. It's taken me a long time to come to terms with this. I tried to chase away the black beast, but he was stronger than I. I tried to transcend the black beast (by taking up transcendental meditation for a spell some twenty-five years ago) but he wouldn't be transcended! Eventually I learned to contain him. He is part of me as I am part of him. He prowls within me. Mostly he's at ease. But sometimes he grows furious. Then he storms and thunders with a fury so terrible it would overwhelm me. I look on, helpless.

At such times I turn to a line of Robert Frost (from his poem 'The Runaway') in which a little Morgan colt who is 'not winter-broken' is terrified of the snow. He bolts. He may run all he likes, but he cannot escape the terror of the snow. Were she with him, his mother, the voice of experience, would advise him with 'Sakes, /It's only weather.' And he'd learn, as I did, to believe that voice. That storms can be weathered. That is Frost's voice. That is my mother's voice. It has taught me a new song. When I am overwhelmed and feel like bolting, I remember 'The Runaway' and stand my ground. I compose

myself in song, turning pain to poetry. Balancing song and terror – a
fair exchange.

I hope you like the poem. Maybe there's someone out there who can
take sustenance, too, from 'Sakes,/It's only weather.' If there is, I hope
s/he comes across this poem. Which is why I give it to you as my
choice.

God bless!

Gabriel Fitzmaurice

The Runaway

Once when the snow of the year was beginning to fall,
We stopped by a mountain pasture to say, 'Whose colt?'
A little Morgan had one fore foot on the wall,
The other curled at his breast. He dipped his head
And snorted at us. And then he had to bolt.
We heard the miniature thunder where he fled,
And we saw him, or thought we saw him, dim and grey
Like a shadow against the curtain of falling flakes.
'I think the little fellow's afraid of the snow.
He isn't winter-broken. It isn't play
With the little fellow at all. He's running away.
I doubt if even his mother could tell him, "Sakes,
It's only weather." He'd think she didn't know!
Where is his mother? He can't be out alone.'
And now he comes again with a clatter of stone,
And mounts the wall again with whited eyes
And all his tail that isn't hair up straight.
He shudders his coat as if to throw off flies.
'Whoever it is that leaves him out so late,
When other creatures have gone to stall and bin,
Ought to be told to come and take him in.'

ROBERT FROST (1874–1963)

MAUREEN GAFFNEY

Dear Marie

Thank you for inviting me to contribute to your book. I am somewhat daunted by the prospect of attempting the task you have set me. Committing to words what gives me spiritual sustenance may sound impossibly portentous, the language of the spirit being beyond words for most of us, except for poets. My choice is Day by Day, *the last collection of poems published by the great American poet Robert Lowell. In many ways, he seems the most unlikely source of spiritual sustenance. He wrote this last collection of poems, in his fifties, as he contemplated, without the consolation of religion, the pain and loss in his own life: being unwanted by his mother; the agonising separations, reconciliation and final ruptures of three failed marriages; mental breakdowns; his emotional distance from his father; the inevitable declines of aging; fear of dying. He died at age 60, a few weeks after the poems were published.*

As a young man, Lowell had embraced his art as a quest for the sublime, writing poems of blazing passion and religious vision, elegantly and formally structured by 'plot and rhyme'. He wanted to make life happen, to create poems that were exquisitely made objects. Now, in late middle age, the striving energy of youth deserts him, or he abandons it, making room for a more reflective energy. In Day by Day, *his 'verse autobiography', he confronts his life, acknowledging his uncertainty, depression, and exhaustion. His last poem 'Epilogue' begins: 'Those blessed structures, plot and rhyme – / why are they no help to me now?'*

His question echoes the spiritual crisis that is forced on us when, at moments of great personal significance, all the striving energy that motivates and shapes our daily struggle to make life happen, for achievement, affirmation, and order, seems to fall away and fail us as an adequate explanation of the truth of what is glimpsed. In my own case, I think immediately of the most intensely personal events that tumbled me, almost by surprise, into awareness of the deeper meaning of what was happening – the birth of my children; my father's death; the pleasure and pain of realising that even in the most intimate relationships, there is always something else to be known about ourselves and each other. I think too of those moments of pure grace when I wanted to still the moment forever – days on family holidays; a teenager, rushing out the door, suddenly turning back to say good-bye: eager, effortlessly affectionate, bursting with life. Such experiences leave me feeling something akin to wonder, or humility, in awe at the inexhaustible abundance of life, and at the same time, its fragility. In his last poem, 'Epilogue', Lowell describes such moments of intense feeling as 'stealing like the tide across a map', illuminating, even sanctifying the ordinary.

In Day by Day *Lowell writes of such ordinary events. Abandoning the fiery certainty and vision of his early work, he, instead, 'pray(s) for the grace of accuracy'. The results are poems of stunning beauty, catching those 'sacramental instants' of daily life. For example, he writes of marriage and domestic life, a subject that does not easily lend to epiphanies. Taking as his subject Van Eyck's portrait of the Arnolfini Marriage: a plain husband, a pregnant wife, surrounded by the normal debris of domestic life: scattered shoes, the 'restless marital canopy'. The portrait is 'too much like their life/ a crisscross, too many petty facts'. But amidst the 'too many petty facts', is the 'miracle of lighting', the 'sacramental instant' that illuminates and gives sustenance to their lives:*

> They are rivals in homeliness and love;
> her hand lit like china in his,
> her other hand
> is in touch with the head of her unborn child.
> They wait and pray,
> as if the airs of heaven
> that blew on them when they married
> were now a common visitation,
> not a miracle of lighting
> for the photographer's sacramental instant.

But it is the last poem he ever wrote, 'Epilogue', that I love the most, his final meditative glance backwards as he moves towards death. In this poem, he harks back to what used to work for him. He rails, temporarily, against the inadequacy of his art to capture the truth of what happens, to make something of his life 'paralyzed by fact'. Temporarily, he despairs 'All's misalliance':

Those blessed structures, plot and rhyme –
why are they no help to me now
I want to make
something imagined, not recalled?
I hear the noise of my own voice:
The painter's vision is not a lens,
it trembles to caress the light.
But sometimes everything I write
with the threadbare art of my eye
seems like a snapshot,
lurid, rapid, garish, grouped,
heightened from life,
yet paralyzed by fact.
All's misalliance.

Faced with the aesthetic and psychological task of making sense of the inevitable disappointments and sadness of a life that seems 'lurid, rapid, garish, grouped', Lowell returns with the most celebratory of lines: 'Yet why not say what happened?' In this final poem, Lowell knows with 'the grace of accuracy' that the miracle of life is the truth of what happens, not the way it might have been, or the way we wished it had been, but the way we are, 'solid with yearning', in the flux and quick of our lives. We are, he warns, 'poor passing facts'. The truth of what happens to us must be recorded before it is gone for ever – 'each figure in the photograph' given 'his living name'.

Yet why not say what happened?
Pray for the grace of accuracy
Vermeer gave to the sun's illumination
stealing like a tide across a map
to his girl solid with yearning.
We are poor passing facts,
warned by that to give
each figure in the photograph
his living name.

Lowell once complained to the literary critic Helen Vendler that people who wrote about him never said what he would like them to say. 'What's that?' she asked him. 'That I'm heartbreaking' he answered . And he is. Wallace Stevens, his fellow American poet, declared that the aim of modern poetry was 'not to console or sanctify but plainly to propound'. In Day by Day *Lowell plainly and*

heartbreakingly propounds. The effect is, paradoxically, profoundly
spiritually sustaining:

> universal consolatory
> description without significance,
> transcribed verbatim with my eye.

Maureen Gaffney

JOHN McKENNA

Dear Marie

I find spiritual sustenance in the everyday things, in the quotidian thing of living, rather than in anything transcendent. I suspect this is explained by my being an atheist, and whilst I respect and admire the faith which comforts and inspires others, such faith means nothing to me and is utterly absent from my life.

This absence has led me on a search for things which delight and create and give pleasure, in music from the great wordsmiths of music, theatre, the great jazz musicians and, recently, the great classical composers. There are the pleasures of literature and painting and, above all, the pleasure and creativity of food and wine.

Working with food and wine, and writing about these subjects and the people who create them, intensifies one's delight in temporal things, for we produce food and make wine precisely in order to consume these things, and therefore appreciating them in their moment of greatest pleasure is the entire point of the pursuit. They are not transcendent, they do not express anything spiritual: they are simply of themselves, and as such they are perfect, from the most humble radish to the most noble wine.

Above all, having the good fortune to fall in love, and to be in love with one's family, is the most transcendent aspect of life, and perhaps something we might describe as spiritual, for such love is unconditional, and if it cannot be explained, it nevertheless is the ultimate aesthetic in the art of living, and it is the factor that can make all of us 'poets of happiness', as someone once described the work of the photographer Jacques Henri Lartigue.

Best wishes with the book

Yours

John McKenna

ANDY POLLAK

He hath showed thee, O man, what is good; and what
doth the Lord require of thee, but to do justly, and to
love mercy, and to walk humbly with thy God?

MICAH 6:8

Whatsoever things are true, whatsoever things are
honest, whatsoever things are just, whatsoever things
are pure, whatsoever things are lovely, whatsover things
are of good report – if there be any virtue, and if there be
any praise, think on these things.

PHILIPPIANS 4:8

Beautiful, beautiful, beautiful God/was breathing his
love by a cutaway bog.

PATRICK KAVANAGH, 'THE ONE'

Dear Marie Heaney

*These two famous biblical verses, one from the Old Testament, one
from the New, are linked together in a prayer in the second order of
worship of the Dublin Unitarian Church. The line from Kavanagh is
from a 1958 poem about God – 'the One and Endless, the Mind that
has baulked the profoundest of mortals'.*

*It is only in recent years that I have again become a (tentative)
believer in God. It is a unitarian – even pantheist – belief in God in
the universe, rather than any attachment to the personal and
trinitarian Christian God I grew up with (although I do try to follow
the teachings of Christ, as by far the best exemplar of a divinely-
inspired life I have ever come across). God, insofar as my puny
intellect and imagination can understand the concept, is the
universal spirit of goodness at work in the world (often in conflict
with a similarly omnipresent spirit of evil). Whenever that spirit of
goodness is revealed, I am spiritually nourished and strengthened.
Thus people's goodness as it shows itself in their acts – great and
small – of justice and solidarity, compassion and kindness, is
infinitely more important to me than faith in God, let alone any
specific dogma about how that faith should be followed. That is why I*

find the prophet Micah's words so inspiring. If more of us obeyed the commandments to justice, mercy and humility before the God of the universe, the world would be an incomparably better place.

Equally, the pantheist in me values truth, honesty, justice, purity and beauty above almost all things (add in gentleness and courage and you have my entire pantheon of virtues). When I get depressed about the rotten state of the world and my rotten weakness in the face of it, I try to do what St Paul advises: 'Think on these things.'

Beauty, and especially beauty in nature, is a particular consolation. Kavanagh saw God in the multi-coloured riot of small spring flowers which appear on the black-brown bogs all over Ireland in the early days of spring. I prefer to look upwards – to the hills, 'from whence cometh my strength', in the psalmist's words. I take inspiration from the dark line of the Dublin hills I am fortunate enough to glimpse from my bedroom window; from walking the snow-flecked winter slopes above Glenmalure in wild south Wicklow; and from contemplation of the vastness and stillness and mystery of mountains everywhere.

I trust these random, utterly unoriginal thoughts will strike an echo somewhere. Thank you for inviting me to take part in your excellent project, which I hope will raise many tens of thousands of pounds for Focus Ireland.

Warmest best wishes

Andy Pollak

'And, as for death itself...Only in India have I felt free of our Western fear of death, and sensed it as part of a greater process, a change of state, an abandoning of a worn out physical husk, perhaps for something else.'

John Montague

'It is true to say that at the moment of death one is more alive than ever... Truth is present: there is no time for sentimentality.'

Mairead Ní Mhaonaigh

'But they that held through winter to the spring
Despair as I do and as I do, sing.'

Hilaire Belloc, quoted by Lelia Doolan

'I know there is no death if we are brave, and thoughtful, and quiet, and know exactly where we are.'

Theo Dorgan

'By being the curators of our images we care for our souls.'

Thomas Moore, quoted by Imogen Stuart

'Jazz is huge. That the suffering and degradation of slavery should bring forth so much redemptive beauty is miraculous.'

Michael Longley

'The late Bedouin King, Hussein, began his political life by witnessing the assassination of his chief (his grandfather) and ended it by weeping over the bodies of the children of his enemies.'

Kathy Sheridan

'No matter... Try again... Fail again... Fail better...'

Samuel Beckett, quoted by Olwen Fouéré

ENDA McDONAGH

Dear Marie

Late and breathless (even spiritless) I send you my piece. It's a letter to the daughter of a friend.

Enda

Letter to Sarah

Dear Sarah

The letter promised on the occasion of your baptism inevitably came to nothing. A fresh promise to write something on 'the sources of spirituality' prompts this further attempt to address your future faith. Topic and title are too daunting for both of us, given the elusiveness of 'spirituality' and the endless possibilities of 'sources'. Ruthless reduction is the only possible strategy so you may have to listen to one more bore's recollections and reflections on what seemed to him significant influences on erratic attempts at real human living in body and spirit.

The reality of people and the risks

Getting real as you might advise your parents has been a lifelong struggle of coming to terms with the reality of people, from parents and siblings to school-mates and colleagues to beloved friends and persistent enemies or at least opponents. In all their different and often ambiguous ways they teach you about life in the Spirit. In the cherished memories life-story is love-story. People one has loved and loves, people who have loved and who still love one in spite of all, are primary sources of whatever we mean by spiritual life. This is certainly true for those who try to follow Jesus' example and command. Your baptism proclaimed as much: you are born and then re-born to a life of love by water and the Holy Spirit. We are able to love in that we are first loved, immediately by family and friends, ultimately by that great spiritual reality, the God who in New Testament terms is love.

The spiritual life then is a life of loving and of being loved and the historical sources are people, rooted for Christians in the tri-personal God of baptism, of Father, Son and Holy Spirit. (The sexist resonance of this language is bound to be a bit off-putting. One of the tasks for your generation will be to get beyond it.)

Of course, people and loving are not problem-free. Ambiguities abound. Destruction threatens as fulfilment is promised. Betrayal shadows fidelity. Best friends may become worst enemies. Fratricide has a depressing history and civil war is reputedly the most savage.

The risks of people and of loving are only too real and too often issue in destruction for them to be ignored. They have to be integrated into the deeper life of the Spirit, the loving, forgiving re-creative life by which such betrayal and destruction may be overcome. By which they were overcome in Jesus. By which they could be overcome by his followers if they were not so inclined to follow their fearful and vengeful instincts. Baptism by water and the Holy Spirit has a transforming, re-creating and loving potential in human life and love – that is why it is spoken of in terms of overcoming original sin, the fearful and vengeful instincts carried by the human community. It is not only the baptised and certainly not always the baptised who manifest this transforming potential. Baptism is its symbol. Loving and forgiving people are its realisation. The forgiving response in the famous example of Gordon Wilson and of many others less famous, remains a true source of spiritual living and loving.

Compassion and its causes

The spiritual is not just discernible in the personal–relational, central as that is. It emerges also in the larger commitments which people undertake for the sake of particular groups of people and communities. It inspires devotion to causes from caring for the sick and the poor to saving the earth, the community of all the living. Truth and beauty, freedom, justice and peace are typical of generic categories of the causes which inspire human spiritual commitment. In reducing mood once more I will focus on compassion and the kinds of causes it generates.

Compassion, basically suffering with, enables one to share the human sufferings and privation which are such a prominent and continuing feature of our world. 'The whole earth is our hospital' in Eliot's words and compassion is essential to its healing. Healing comes from within person and community. Compassion is the *cead isteach*. The permission to enter. In the Christian tradition, that permission was sought by God from Mary and by Jesus from the excluded and deprived with whom he would establish his new *koinonia*, the new healed and healing human community.

The several causes of a single life-time prove nourishing and frustrating. The wounded healer is frequently healed but incurs new wounds also. Causes enlarge, energise and renew. They can also delude, deceive and sometimes destroy. The free commitment to the great causes can become imprisoning obsessions in which people, the usual origin and test of the cause, are obscured and even abused. Great causes, religious and political, necessary as they are to humanity's breathing Spirit, must at best endure partial failure. At worst they may destroy the cause's promoters and its would-be beneficiaries. This century, even this short life-time, has seen some horrific example of causes going wrong. That is why causes always need compassion just as compassion to be widely effective must organise itself about particular causes: fighting famine, promoting peace, preventing HIV/AIDS at particular times in particular places for very particular people.

Creations and discoveries

The human spirit is restless in search of new developments, new expressions, new discoveries. Artistic creation and scientific discovery bear witness to the reach of that restless spirit. For the less gifted in those areas, the observers, readers and learners rather than the creators and discoverers, entering into the works of the gifted, or better, allowing these works to enter into them has its own transforming, liberating and healing effects.

One's spirit, one's self is set free, renewed and healed. In the present high-energy state of artistic Ireland, despite its variable standards and inevitable pretensions, the spiritual possibilities are many. Creativity carries its ambiguities but, as a state of mind, encourages us beyond ourselves even if we then fall flat on our faces.

The risks of creating haunt every artist even as they haunted Eliot's 'ruined millionaire' who endowed the earth. Self-exposure into self-transcendence would be apt summary of human and divine creation in which we all share in some limited fashion. It characterises life in the Spirit at so many levels from love and friendship to the greatest artistic achievement. Haunted by words as we are it is exhilarating to realise that finding and discovery have a Latin equivalent, *invenere*, which issues in our word for inventing and making (creating). The thrills of discovery which the great scientists (and archaeologists and explorers) enjoy are open to their students and followers. In our world, where such work has been seen as so different from that of the artists, it is important to stress the imaginative leaps in scientific discovery and inventing, and the discovering, coming-upon dimension of artistic achievement. What Richard Wilbur described as letting a poem happen to him reflects the giftedness which many poets and scientists, politicians and religious people experience in their best endeavours, their most spiritual activities.

On the threshold of contemplation

Faced with the give and the gift, finding a way to understand and express it, the spiritual in us may pause to rest in the gift and in achievement of understanding and expressing. For the restless human spirit in a distracted world the resting is not easy. At its deepest, that rest is silence and demands silence. And silence is risky, too risky for most of us most of the time and so we rush back to noisy thinking and talking and acting. Yet the people and the causes, the poems and the paintings and the scientific discoveries, summon us at times to silence. Not least the silence of awe and wonder at 'the achieve of, the mastery of the thing'. In a lifetime of gratitude and regrets one of the most serious regrets is the repeated hesitancy on the edge of silence, on the threshold of contemplation. Perhaps your generation, Sarah, maturing through and beyond the distractions of the age may find the courage and skill to cross that threshold.

The risk of God

Crossing the threshold poses particular threats for would-be Christians. It involves the risk of God. Institutionalised and domesticated, ritualised and even sacramentalised God remains mainly undisturbing, unchallenging. The comfort-blanket God, providing irrational therapy for those who refuse to grow up, is a common enough distortion. The real God of creation and incarnation, of crucifixion and resurrection is seldom risked.

The self-exposure involved seems too painful, and fruitless to boot. The promised self-transcendence no longer sounds persuasive. And yet all the other self-exposures addressed here, from love and friendship through compassion and its causes to creation and discovery, hold a promise that incites trust that is of course sometimes betrayed but not always and, further trust, not for ever.

In later years I have become more conscious of our need to risk God, to follow the line of self-exposure into self-transcendence, or more accurately self-surrender. Human experiences have encouraged this mood and move. More recently a growing sense of the risks taken by the originator ('the ruined millionaire') in creating, in entering into compassionate companionship with the earth and its peoples has driven me to risk a little more of myself in the silence, in the darkness, so well described in the spiritual and mystical traditions.

If you ever get this far, Sarah, you will undoubtedly be forgiving of an older man's ramblings and vague memories. Too vague indeed for the more concrete illustrations of a life-story that makes a botched love-story in search of a healing ending.

Slán agus beannacht

Enda

MARY FINAN

Dear Marie

I derive my spiritual sustenance from beaches, mountains, music and love.

One of the most calming experiences on this earth is the sound of water. It heals the mind and soothes the soul. Walking on a deserted beach in peaceful solitude clears away all stress. It fills me with the pure joy of living. Irish beaches are best, and Curracloe in County Wexford is the most beautiful of all. It must be the Celt in me that cannot find the same sustenance in those creamy Caribbean beaches!

The Dublin mountains offer the same restorative and uplifting powers. Often, when I am sad or low, I will go there and drink in the wild beauty of it all. But it is not always possible to get away, so now I have brought the mountains to my office in the form of a wonderful painting by Eugene Conway. It faces my desk and never fails to restore my equilibrium.

As the years pass by, music has become more and more important to me. In a world beleaguered by famine, war and unbearable personal tragedy, it reassures me about the nobility of man who can reach such sublime perfection.

But perhaps I would not be capable of deriving such an abundance of spiritual sustenance from all these things if I were not nourished by so many loving relationships. I am blessed with a large circle of family and friends who have generously shared my sorrows and joys throughout my life and whose very existence is sufficient to make me believe in a good and gentle God.

Yours

Mary Finan

MARY O'MALLEY

Dear Marie Heaney

Thank you for your kind invitation. Can I mention both a poem and a song as I could no more do without one than the other?

'On Angels' by Czeslaw Milosz is a poem of great faith in the inner life and perception of human beings. I turn to it often and it clears my mind like a mantra.

> The voice – no doubt it is a valid proof,
> as it can belong only to radiant creatures,
> weightless and winged (after all, why not?),
> girdled with the lightning

It is the bracketed question, with its wit and its intelligence and insistence on the visionary, that draws me back to the poem again and again, along with its final injunction:

> day draws near
> another one
> do what you can.

Music, both played and sung, seems to me to be the natural language of the spirit and in Irish, its highest expression is often to be found in the lament.

'Caoineadh na dTri Muire' is an intimate and moving lament for the death of Christ, transposed from distant Calvary to the immediate locality of the singer by the intimacy and power of the language. Seosamh Ó hÉanaí, the great Conamara sean nós singer who died in America in the 1980s recorded a version of this lament that gives it its full incantatory power, based as it is on a tradition where to sing was to survive and faith had much to do with the observance and tensions of inherited shape and form. I don't listen to it often but I hear cadences familiar from across the generations when I do and that seems to be important in a way I cannot, and do not need to define.

Mary O'Malley

On Angels

All was taken away from you: white dresses,
wings, even existence.
Yet I believe you,
messengers.

There, where the world is turned inside out,
a heavy fabric embroidered with stars and beasts,
you stroll, inspecting the trustworthy seams.

Short is your stay here:
now and then at a matinal hour, if the sky is clear,
in a melody repeated by a bird,
or in the smell of apples at the closte of day
when the light makes the orchards magic.

They say somebody has invented you
but to me this does not sound convincing
for humans invented themselves as well.

The voice – no doubt it is a valid proof,
as it can belong only to radiant creatures,
weightless and winged (after all, why not?),
girdled with the lightning

I have heard that voice many a time when asleep
and, what is strange, I understood more or less
an order or an appeal in an unearthly tongue:

day draws near
another one
do what you can.

CZESLAW MILOSZ (1911–)

Caoineadh na dTrí Muire

'A Pheadair, a Aspail, an bhfaca tú mo ghrá geal?'
        M'ochón agus m'ochón Ó
'Chonaic mé ar ball é i láthair a namhad.'
        M'ochón agus m'ochón Ó

'Gabhaigí i leith, a dhá Mhuire, go gcaoine sibh mo ghrá geal.'
        M'ochón agus m'ochón Ó

'Céard tá le chaoineadh againn, muna gcaoinimid a
chnámha?'
 M'ochón agus m'ochón Ó

'Cé hé an fear breá sin ar chrann na Páise?
 M'ochón agus m'ochón Ó
'An é nach n-aithníonn tú do Mhac, a Mháthair?'
 M'ochón agus m'ochón Ó

'Agus an é sin an Maicín a d'iompair me trí ráithe?'
 M'ochón agus m'ochón Ó
'Nó an é sin an Maicín a rugadh sa stábla?'
 M'ochón agus m'ochón Ó

'Nó an é sin an Maicín a hoileadh in ucht Mháire?'
 M'ochón agus m'ochón Ó
'Mhaise, éist, a Mháithrín, is ná bí cráite.'
 M'ochón agus m'ochón Ó

'Agus an é sin an casúir a bhuail tríot na tairní?'
 M'ochón agus m'ochón Ó
'Nó an í sin an tsleá a chuaigh trí do lár geal?'
 M'ochón agus m'ochón Ó

'Nó an í sin an choróin spíonta chuaigh ar do mhullach
álainn?'
 M'ochón agus m'ochón Ó
'Mhaise, éist, a Mháithrín, is ná bí cráite.'
 M'ochón agus m'ochón Ó

'Atá mná mo chaointe le breith go fóilleach.'
 M'ochón agus m'ochón Ó
'Mhaise, éist, a Mháithrín, is ná bí cráite.'
 M'ochón agus m'ochón Ó

'Níl aon duine chaoinfeas Thú in ioleán Pharrthais.'
 M'ochón agus m'ochón Ó
'Ba gheal í a leaba i bhFlaithis na ngrásta.'
 M'ochón agus m'ochón Ó

TRADITIONAL

PAUL ANDREWS

Dear Marie

As a contribution to your anthology, I am choosing a piece from Barjona. *In the autumn of 1940 the Nazis captured and deported Jean-Paul Sartre, the existentialist philosopher and playwright, to a concentration camp in Germany. Before Christmas a Jesuit fellow prisoner, Paul Feller, persuaded Jean-Paul to write a nativity play for the French Christians who shared his captivity. Sartre, baptised a Catholic, was by this time a declared atheist. Writing a Christian play ran against the grain. But as a gesture of solidarity with his French fellow-prisoners, he wrote* Barjona, Jeu Scénique en six tableaux.

To my knowledge the play was never published in Sartre's lifetime. Presumably, Sartre saw it as a jeu d'esprit, *like a piece written for a Christmas party among friends. As an atheist and existentialist, he would not appreciate its location in a spiritual anthology. However, the play is of such searing beauty that whenever I have quoted it, people have looked for the text and marvelled.*

Barjona is the headman of a village near Bethlehem at the time of Jesus' birth. He is a Sartre-like figure, a strong man consumed by existentialist despair. The villagers are starving and powerless under the yoke of Rome, and he cannot help them. In the play he has just persuaded his fellow-villagers into a joint pact that they will bring no more children into the world, in protest against the oppression of Rome and the silence of God. Then the Magi enter, following a star. Barjona abuses them as doting, deluded old men, and points to the misery of the crowd who have gathered, torn between despair and hope. Baith, one of the wise men from the East, answers Barjona with gravity:

> You see this man here, weighed down with his flesh,
> rooted on the spot by his two big feet, and you say,
> pointing your finger to touch him, *he is there* – but that
> is not true. Wherever a man is, Barjona, he is always
> somewhere else. Somewhere beyond the purple
> peaks that you see over there by Jerusalem, beyond
> this icy day, in a tomorrow. And these people

standing round you, for quite a while now they are
not there any more. They are at Bethlehem, in a
stable, round the little warm body of a baby. And all
this future of which man is moulded, all these peaks,
these purple horizons, these wonderful towns, which
he haunts without ever having set foot there, that is
hope.

*(Here you must imagine the French prisoners speaking their lines in
a concentration camp.)*

Look at the prisoners before you, who live in mud
and in cold. Do you know what you could see if you
could follow their souls? Hills, and the sweet
meanderings of a river, and vines, and the sun of the
south, their vines and their sun. It is down there that
you will find them. And those gilded vines of
September, for a prisoner who is shivering and full of
vermin, that is hope. Hope is the best part of
themselves. You want to deprive them of their vines
and their meadows and their shining distant hills.
You want to give them the bewildering present of the
beast.

There is your despair, to ruminate on the instant that
passes, to gaze between your toes with a stupid and
rancorous eye, to tear your soul from the future and
imprison it in the present. Then you will no longer be
a man, Barjona. You will be no better than a hard
black stone on the road. The caravans pass on the
road, but the stone stays alone, fixed like mud in its
resentment.

Barjona: You're doting, you old fool.

Baith: Barjona, it is true that we are very old and very
wise and we know all the evil in the world. Still,
when we saw this star in heaven, our hearts leaped
for joy like the hearts of children. We have been like
children, and we set out on the road because we
wanted to accomplish our duty as men, the duty of
hope. The man who loses hope, Barjona, will be
chased from his village, and cursed. The stones of the
road will be rougher under his feet and the brambles

more spiky. The load will weigh heavier on his back,
all his misfortunes will plague him like angry bees,
and everyone will mock him. But everything smiles
on the man who hopes. For him the world is a gift.
Come on then, see if you want to stay here or make
up your mind to follow us.

*Later in his career Sartre took issue with the psychoanalysts of Paris.
'There is no such thing as the Unconscious,' he wrote. 'There is only
bad faith.' As I read these incomparable images of hope, I wonder
where they came from: did his Unconscious aspire to something
better than the brute present?*

The existence and plot of the play Barjona *is as intriguing as the text
is beautiful. After meeting the Magi, the villagers follow them to
Bethlehem in search of the new-born King. Barjona, determined to
eliminate this illusion before it catches the imagination of his friends,
takes a short cut over the mountains to Bethlehem, where he plans to
kill the baby. There is a gap in the text – Sartre's note reads: 'Il
manque trois pages' – before it resumes in the stable. Barjona is on
his knees, watching from the shadows as the villagers gather round
the manger. Sartre will not describe a conversion, but he leaves the
door open for hope.*

*The typescript came my way from a French fellow-student in
Munich, shortly after the war. Fr Feller had given him a copy. Our
life in Munich was spartan. I was cold, hungry (the basic diet was
still turnips and potatoes) and, as an isolated Irishman, lonely. I
needed hope, not as a theological virtue, but as an existential
experience, to help me trust that there was something beyond this
stark and loveless existence.*

We put on Barjona *as a radio play one Christmas. It was not like
spiritual books which spoke from a faith too comfortable and
unquestioning. I responded to Sartre when he described the
Incarnation: 'a god who would submit to learning this taste of salt at
the bottom of our mouths when the whole world abandons us'. This
was philosophy from the guts, not the head. It gave me spiritual
sustenance when I needed it most. It has stood to me in bad times
since then, recalling me to 'our duty as humans, the duty of hope'.*

Thank you for the excuse to recall it.

Paul Andrews SJ

DEIRDRE PURCELL

Dear Marie

My father knew I was an agnostic and I am sure this caused him some, or much pain.

Bill was my father.

He was a righteous Roman Catholic but Christian also – in that he never upbraided me, nor raised the subject of my meandering sub-beliefs.

On the 26th February, 1999, one month from the date on which I write this, the television was switched off just before the nine o'clock news and the curtains were swished around all the beds in the abruptly silent ward. Bill was about to die. The young hospital chaplain, sensing that I, at least, was not open to orthodox comforting concerning ascents to heaven, spoke to my brother and me. Bill lives on, he told us. His spirit lives in everyone who ever met him, thought about him, loved him, or came under his influence.

Bill is my father.

In the aftermath of his death, I came across the following, from Teilhard de Chardin.

> That success may crown our enterprises, joy dwell in our hearts and all around us, and what sorrow we cannot be spared, can be transfigured into a finer joy, the joy of knowing that we have occupied our own station in the universe and that in that station, we have done as we ought...

Bill occupied his station in the universe. I hope I will too.

Deirdre Purcell

THEO DORGAN

Dear Marie

I have no formal religious or spiritual practice in my life. When put on the spot I sometimes describe myself as a freelance pagan Buddhist, but it would be perhaps more accurate to say that my spiritual life, which is all my life, is a thing of epiphanic bursts linked fore-and-aft by the premonitory light or the afterglow.

MacDiarmid's poem I encountered first when I heard him read it in Cork during my days there as a student. It was like a grenade bursting in my head, the sense of immediate confrontation with death, with mystery – '… the last wild look ye gied/afore ye deed!' – and then the human softening of 'foolish licht', the thoughtful, murmuring close of 'what your look meant then'. Beautiful, I thought, realising that the beautiful can be blunt, terrifying and fearless. It's all there in the wild look, the shocked stare as knowledge, real knowledge, flares in the mind, flashes in the eyes.

Long afterwards and since I wondered at the way in which this poem stuck so fast in my mind. Technically it's a single bravura flourish, a thing turned on the wrist, a gesture. But I don't know another poem that looks death sharp in the face, unflinching in its economy, as this poem does, and I comfort my soul with that opening out into common, thoughtful humanity which is its after-echo. I sense, too, the great halls of space and time against which, in which, this tiny and all-too-human drama is played out, and I say the poem over to myself once more and I am not afraid, and I am not alone. When I feel myself most in love, and so most acutely aware that we must die, I hear this poem somewhere in my mind and I look into her eyes and I know there is no death if we are brave, and thoughtful, and quiet, and know exactly where we are.

Love
Theo

The Watergaw

Ae weet forenicht i' yow-trummle
I saw yon antrin thing,
A watergaw wi' its chitterin' licht
Ayont the on-ding;
An' I thocht o' the last wild look ye gied
Afore ye deed!

There was nae reek i' the laverock's hoose
That nicht – an' nane i' mine;
But I hae thocht o' that foolish licht
Ever sin' syne;
An' I think that mebbe at last I ken
What your look meant then.

HUGH McDIARMID (1892–1978)

watergaw – indistinct rainbow; weet – wet; forenicht – evening; yow-
trummle – cold weather after sheep shearing; antrin – rare; chitterin'
– shivering; on-ding – onset (or driving rain or sleet); reek – smoke;
laverock's – lark's

CIARÁN BENSON

Dear Marie

What has given me 'spiritual sustenance'? Presumably this has to do with something that nourishes and sustains 'my spirit'. But what might that mean? There is nothing simple about the meaning of 'spirit', and actually the meaning of 'my' is, I suspect, even more difficult. And yet I know what the question is getting at, but only because we share so much taken-for-granted understanding. To answer the question is in some sense to give an account of myself, and that of course will vary from one time to the next throughout the course of my life. But it is possible to identify some of the features that shape this aspect of my own lifescape, incomplete though that map might be. Perhaps it would be helpful, given that the question is so personal, if I begin with a general point about how I think of human being *and then zone in on what I found nourishes me. Since your question is a serious one, forgive the time it takes to sketch an answer to it. Pedantry as the entrance ticket to the personal!*

As human beings living our precarious time-limited lives, facing crises that threaten our abilities to continue and to cope, we know that without certain dimensions to our lives the outcomes for us could be more uncertain still, more painful than they are. Part of the problem for us is time itself, and it is our felt understanding of 'our' time that roots hope and despair. Part of the problem also is the apparently infinite creativity of natural languages, and our general human capacity to take almost anything as standing for something else. These extraordinary capacities for symbolisation which characterise Homo sapiens sapiens *– our species with its life of maybe a hundred thousand years occupies a mere moment in cosmic time – present each of us with the very powers that sustain but may also destroy us. These are powers of imagining what is not but might be, or of believing that what was need not have been. These are the powers that give rise to love and hate, to acceptance and condemnation, to creative openness or arid closure. They are the roots of our capacity for self-transcendence, but may also serve to thwart it.*

What strikingly distinguishes human beings from all other

creatures, including genetically similar fellow-primates like the chimpanzees, is our capacity to create culture. Culture rests on a fundamental fact about creatures like us: we are essentially social beings who talk and make meanings. Built into our genes, into our origination as a species and as persons, into our minds and into our lives are these facts of 'togetherness', 'talk' and 'meaning'. This is what makes us what we are, and also gives us what limited and variable powers we may have to make something of ourselves. Culture is what enables this to happen, granted a normal biology. The hallmark of culture is the accumulation *over generations of artefacts of all kinds (including tools of language and thought). It encompasses the products of these tools and an understanding of how to use them. It includes stories which make and maintain the sense that we have of ourselves as this kind of people rather than that kind.*

Across the generations and across the world, across history and place, different problems confront human beings, new understandings are constructed, distinctive cultures arise and fall. One fact that all cultures must face is that our hold on time is transient, that death is the great inevitability for every one of us and for our cultures, and that feelings of loss and grief are universal. Every culture must tell a story about this, and the telling of that narrative begins in early childhood.

My culture told its story to me when I was a child in the 1950s in Dún Laoghaire. That story became a warm, intimate part of me, became 'me' and 'mine', shaped how I saw the world, objectified the 'soul' it said was my essence, and instructed me on how to nourish and sustain it. It built into me emotions that acted as control systems for being the sort of kid that the 1950s Irish Christian Brothers' Catholic Story idealised. I took it seriously and in time I made my exit from that story and from its tellers for equally serious reasons.

From a child's perspective the 1950s were a curiously still time as I remember. Now I know how economically, socially and culturally bereft that decade was. But some of the signs of that poverty were what I came to love. Nature quickly reclaimed spaces vacated by people. Big houses without occupants around Dún Laoghaire became places to explore, where wood pigeons might nest on a stairwell, or buddleias root in a leaking parapet. Once impeccable gardens grew wild, paint flaked, lawns became meadows. Birds, animals, insects, plants recolonised the world, and the balance between human energies and the passing of time seemed evenly balanced. The sea was always there, lapping or slapping against the granite piers, sometimes so still that you could stare for ages trying to see fish or just be mesmerised by the ebb and flow of the weed just below the surface. Again the transience of all before the power of nature was there to be sensed in the crumbling little harbour wall at Scotsman's Bay, or the rotting bulwarks for ships that would never come again.

Churches seemed dustier then because in the shafts of sunlight you could see how suddenly full of particles the otherwise empty air was. The clink of thuribles, the tinkle of the little triple bell at the Consecration, the smell of incense, the light through stained glass, the cool feel of early morning air on the way to serve Mass, the mumble of prayers in Latin, the colour of vestments in an otherwise grey and brown sartorial world, the sense of being in a sacred place suffused by 'The Holy,' and then the silence again – 'Elected Silence, sing to me/And beat upon my whorlèd ear' – these were the sustaining elements of the story told as I felt and lived it. The sense of all this has never left me, and still shapes some regions of my desire. But now I understand more clearly how the appeal of each of these elements, separately and together, was profoundly aesthetic, and how the coalescence of the natural and the aesthetic could yield a subsequent love of the world that might tenuously be called pantheistic.

This Edenic strand of my own cultural story in 1950s Ireland was wrapped together with a much darker one. This was not the direct reason that I subsequently resigned my part in this version of the Catholic story but it indirectly gave me impetus to question its power over me and its values as they shaped life as I felt it then. Power and alienation lay at the dynamic heart of this dark strand. Only 'my' Church knew best, and within my Church only those who were entitled to could speak with authority. As it happened, my Church in my country was the centre of Truth in a decadent secular world. We were embattled but we were confident in our certainty. We were, in fact, what today would probably be called fundamentalist. What I remember with a chill is my own feeling of self-righteousness. But there were problems.

The story penetrated every corner of my life. My body was not my own since it was before all else 'the Temple of the Holy Ghost'. My privacy was not my own since God was all-seeing and omnipresent. My inner thoughts were not to be my own since those that were 'bad' were planted by the devil, and their antibodies – aspirations like little semantic exorcists chanting in the face of the bad thoughts – were there courtesy of the powers of Light and Goodness. And there was always my ubiquitous shadow, my very own Guardian Angel whose loyalties must surely be divided and unreliable.

In adolescence it came to feel like I was adrift on a churning sea and that my only salvation was Faith, that trust which meant accepting without question what the 'proper authorities' told me. To ask the wrong questions, which meant to have the audacity to ask certain questions at all, was to risk being a 'pseudo-intellectual'. Our bodies with their leanings towards pleasure were the weak points and had to be 'mortified'. Matt Talbot with his chains and Dominic Savio with the stones in his bed were offered as role-models. This entire explosive mixture ignited with the sparks of sexual desire. The authority of fear contaminated sexuality and every effort was made to recruit the basic emotions of shame and disgust to control it. As it happens some of our mentors' inability to control their own sexuality – abuse was in evidence – introduced that other serpent into the supposed idyll of embattled certitude, hypocrisy. More than anything else the manifest hypocrisy was what led to my 'apostasy'. The recipes in the story for a good life, even on its terms, simply did not seem to work if the lives of some of its most insistent proponents were anything to go by.

I began to trust what I witnessed rather than what I was told, but then I had to confront the fact that how I made sense of what I now saw largely comprised the ways of thinking I had already been taught. For a while I sought one form of ideological certainty to replace the other. The intolerance of ambiguity and of justified uncertainty took a long time to dissipate and be replaced with an easier acceptance. The reordering of my emotional life when I consciously began to live within the span of just one human life – 'mine' – rather than within the span of 'eternity', was quite a challenge. From the perspective of the eternal, this effort was, at the very least, misguided. From my perspective, it was liberation, and that feeling has never left me, although the challenge of making sense of things is all the greater when the comfort of blind trust in authority is left behind. Much of that existential task is about taking responsibility.

One of the things that struck me in my first storied life was how all things good had their source in God and all things bad in the Devil. When a person behaved well it was because she (actually always 'he' in that patriarchal world) was open to the flow of divine goodness; when a person behaved badly, it was because human weakness – something to be emphatically ashamed of – allowed the Devil scope to enter human history. Human beings were cracks in time, Them looking in benignly or malignantly, Us looking out at the life to come on the other side. The human person was a proxy battleground for other gods' wars, much as it was for the Greeks and Romans.

Encountering Existentialism in my late teens was hugely important, with its emphasis on choice and human freedom. I noticed very clearly that all the distinctive features of human being, both the capacities for good and for evil, were effortlessly given away to supernatural beings by the orthodox religions I knew. I especially came to resent the idea that human courage, generosity, and morality generally were sourced to gods and not to mankind itself, fragile and capricious as humanity might be. Why could we not take responsibility for ourselves and our doings, and with that the credit for developing ways of living well? If we did so with courage, the burden of that responsibility, if grasped with understanding and imagination, would be sobering. It would inject an urgency into how we dealt with the affairs of this life. It would compel us to take care of ourselves and our world since no divinity could be relied upon to do it. We would feel the precariousness of our position in time and take responsibility to protect it.

I now see how my own transition from one account of the world to the other was part of the zeitgeist which has favoured cultural liberation, environmental respect, human rights including rights to freedom of thought and expression, and opportunities for the admiration and tolerance of world views different from my own.

So what type of spirit am I now and what type of sustenance have I felt in need of? I now see the human world as precisely that, the human world. I recognise that a desire for transcendence is a pervasive part of being human. My difficulty is with some accounts of what this desire means and entails. I don't harbour the view that those who take a different path to mine are wrong, as I might have decades ago. I simply accept them as different, so long as they don't violate other people's rights. The reason why I don't find the stories of institutional religions compelling is that I can find no evidence in *my own experience to confirm the existence of a* personal *God, nor of the kinds of providential concern with human life and its future that such beliefs carry with them.*

On the other hand, it is obvious that we are fragile creatures caught up in great cosmic forces that science searches to understand and the arts to express. It may well be that as a species there are phenomena that we are simply not bright enough to understand, like consciousness, or the nature of the origins of the universe. But at the moment an optimistic faith in the powers of human understanding seems like a good policy. If you tell me that I am part of a great unified cosmic order and that you call this an impersonal God, or Tao, then I would find this sort of pantheism plausible.

But the universe is an infinitely vast cold place, as Pascal felt only too clearly, and the thought that I will soon cease to exist utterly and for ever as a person can seem like a terrifying prospect. But what makes it so?

This is where I draw sustenance from my à la carte *Buddhism. I think that little has surpassed the earliest Buddhist account of the roots of human suffering. This understands suffering as resting in human desire. Desire attempts to fix or repeat what is inherently transient and therefore can never be held still or repeated. Suffering is the feeling of pain when this attempt to permanently grasp the object of desire fails, as fail it must. The solution rests in forms of detachment and non-attachment as techniques for cutting the roots of desire and therefore the resulting suffering sustained by desire. As a matter of fact I think this is a workable psychological understanding of suffering and its control.*

I also like the early Buddhist distrust of authorities and institutions. I don't believe in a trans-life karma, in reincarnation, or in the baroque accretions and rituals that have smothered Buddhism over its long travels through history. For myself, I have decided not to cut the roots of desire such that the only way to live in the world is as an ascetic, much as I admire ascetics. I love the world and want to renounce my hold on it only when I must. If I have no foreknowledge of my own death, the terror I mentioned above will not happen. If I do have time to prepare, then I know from experience that the terror is rooted in imagination and that the solution to that is an intense grounding in the only time that does exist, the present. All else is fantasy.

I like the Zen idea of 'suchness.' Not everything need be as it is, nor should many things be allowed to be as they are. But that nothing is fixed and that nothing lasts are insights of which it really can be said 'Such is the world.' These are the terms of life, and knowing them conditions a respect for our own and for the lives of others. To gratuitously end the life of another person seems to me to indicate a profound failure of imagination, to be in a sense already dead to a vital possibility in oneself.

I use the word 'spirit' for the part of me that loves and wants to love. Love is what makes me want to be part of another person or thing and to want them to be part of me. Hate makes others become part of me also but not in a way that I would want. Heraclitus in one of his fragments tells us that 'It is hard to fight with anger: for what it wants it buys at the price of the soul.' This is why victimhood is such a struggle since it imports the seeds of destruction at two levels: the immediate damage caused by the oppressor, and the collateral task of overcoming the ensuing hate and having to fight the tendency to be a hate-full person. Love also puts me at risk of change. Its precondition is openness to the other person or thing. Its means is language in the wider sense. Language and love are media of self-transcendence. This lies at the heart of human creativity.

If I had to choose two books which helped me come to understand some of these things, and which as a matter of fact sustained me at various points in my life in the face of transience and threat, these in particular come to mind. They are simply written but wise. I bought the first when I was about twenty. It was a compilation by Thomas Merton called The Way of Chuang Tzu. *Chuang Tzu was a Taoist thinker who lived over 2300 years ago in China. Meeting him in this was like a breath of fresh air. His wisdom is light, funny, unsystematic and tolerant. I often re-read it and give one short example:*

Three in the Morning

When we wear out our minds, stubbornly clinging to one partial view of things, refusing to see a deeper agreement between this and its complementary opposite, we have what is called 'three in the morning'.

What is this 'three in the morning'?

A monkey trainer went to his monkeys and told them: 'As regards your chestnuts: you are going to have three measures in the morning and four in the afternoon.'

At this they all became angry. So he said: 'All right, in that case I will give you four in the morning and three in the afternoon.' This time they were satisfied.

The two arrangements were the same in that the number of chestnuts did not change. But in one case the animals were displeased, and in the other they were satisfied. The keeper had been willing to change his personal arrangement in order to meet objective conditions. He lost nothing by it!

The truly wise man, considering both sides of the question without partiality, sees them both in the light of Tao.

This is called following two courses at once.

Over ten years later I came across the second book. It is The Dhammapada *and is a collection of over 400 aphorisms from about 2300 years ago presenting the Buddhist moral system or Dhamma.*

Again I give a few examples to convey its flavour. While I dip into it, selectively as with everything else, I think it is a wise, beautiful and helpful account of the human spirit from one point of view:

1   What we are today comes from our thoughts of yesterday, and our present thoughts build our life of tomorrow: our life is the creation of our mind. If a man speaks or acts with an impure mind, suffering follows him as the wheel of the cart follows the beast that draws the cart.

33   The mind is wavering and restless, difficult to guard and restrain: let the wise man straighten his mind as a maker of arrows makes his arrows straight.

49   As the bee takes the essence of a flower and flies away without destroying its beauty and perfume, so let the sage wander in this life.

50   Just as a flower which seems beautiful and has colour but has no perfume, so are the fruitless words of the man who speaks them but does them not.

71   A wrong action may not bring its reaction at once, even
      as fresh milk turns not sour at once: like a smouldering
      fire concealed under ashes it consumes the wrongdoer,
      the fool.

100 Better than a thousand useless words is one single word
      that gives peace.

147 Consider this body! A painted puppet with jointed
      limbs, sometimes suffering and covered with ulcers, full
      of imaginings, never permanent, for ever changing.

155 Those who in their youth did not live in self-harmony,
      and who did not gain the true treasures of life, are later
      like long-legged old herons standing sad by a lake
      without fish.

*My 'spirit' would not be without my body, nor would it be if I
physically managed to survive as an infant and develop outside of
human society and culture. Both determine it. But the limits of my
'spirit' are the limits of my imagination, and since language is
infinitely creative, this suggests that my imagination, as long as my
body allows me to imagine, is largely unbounded. In this sense my
spirit is potentially transcendent, if bounded by the span of my life
and the subsequent life of what I make. What nourishes and sustains
my understanding and my imagination sustains my spirit. For me,
then, 'the true treasures of life' are friendship and love, the natural
world, the arts, a balance in work – very difficult to sustain –
between questing and satisfaction, and laughter. I believe we face
death as we have faced life, and that if there is meaning to the idea of
karma it is a karma within a life and not between this and other lives.
That is because I believe that each and every life happens but once.
Hence the horror of wantonly and irreversibly destroying another's
life, or avoidably diminishing its quality.*

*Osip Mandelstam, in the last verse of one of his final poems before
disappearing for ever into Stalin's Gulag, bequeathes this:*

> And I would like to say to you,
> My little one, mumbling:
> It's by means of our babbling
> That I hand you to the light.

Every best wish

Ciarán Benson

NIALL O'DOWD

Dear Marie

Thank you for your invitation to take part in the book. It sounds like an excellent undertaking.

As an Arts student in University College Dublin in the early 1970s I became friendly with the late Alan Bliss, Professor of English, who became a mentor and a close friend who had a lasting influence on me.

During our occasional drinking sessions he would often quote lines from the English poet AC Swinburne. I don't recall the name of the poem but the words have stayed with me all my life and I often recite them in quiet moments. There is a world-weariness yet a peaceable sense about them that is very attractive to me.

The lines from the poem 'even the weariest river winds somewhere safe to sea' I find immensely reassuring; that despite the traumas of life there is always a road that leads home and ultimately a passage to a different existence. Here are the lines that I remember. I hope I am quoting them accurately:

> From too much love of living from hope and fear set free
> I thank with brief thanksgiving whatever Gods there be
> That no life lives forever that dead men rise up never
> And even the weariest river winds somewhere safe to sea
> I am weary of days and hours, blown buds of barren flowers
> Desire and dreams and powers and everything but sleep

Sometimes in the midst of the hustle and bustle of Manhattan where everything seems so hurried, yet so ephemeral, I find myself reciting them, almost as a mantra.

Thank you for the opportunity.

Niall O'Dowd

OLIVIA O'LEARY

Dear Marie

It was an unusual and interesting brief you gave, and I had to think a bit about it.

Yours sincerely

Olivia O'Leary

The Lilies of the Field

Some truths are delivered to us only by time. For me, it was the knowledge that we are each of us unique and therefore uniquely valuable. The fact that we *are*, is more important than what we *do*.

This wasn't a lesson easily learned. In the Catholic credit/debit analysis of life, one was taught to place good deeds and indulgences against sins and weakness, hoping to remain spiritually in the black. For a scholarship girl like me, effort rewarded became a way of life. Achievements were cashed in return for respect and even affection.

Society loves achievers, but the constant need to achieve becomes tedious and ultimately destructive: I do, therefore I am. But what if I can't do? How do I justify my existence? What if I'm old, or sick, or mad? A society which puts too much emphasis on achievement demotes the helpless and implicitly condones attitudes which can lead to eugenics and even involuntary euthanasia. It undermines the whole basis of what we call civilised values. And it also misses the point.

When my mother was ill, I came on her one day, half asleep, the cat half asleep on her lap. The afternoon sun shone on them both. My mother had done nothing. Neither had the cat. Yet between them, they had created a moment of perfection, of total acceptance. This, too, was an achievement.

There isn't a great deal in scripture which makes sense to me now, but one line from St Luke's Gospel becomes more vivid every day. It says everything I need to know about life and being:

Consider the lilies, how they grow: they toil not, they spin not, and yet I say unto you that Solomon in all his glory was not arrayed like one of these.

LUKE 12: 27

IAN FOX

Dear Marie

Thank you for thinking of me for the new Lifelines-style book. I am always glad to help Focus Ireland.

My belief in the life hereafter as espoused by Western European churches has been diminishing over the years, now close to the point of invisibility. The total ineffectiveness of the organised churches in achieving lasting peace on this island, their ostrich-like attitude to modern humanity, the widening gap between unbending dogma and the real world, and the revelations of there being just too many rotten apples in the barrel, have stretched my credibility so that I no longer care whether they are right or not. I just do not want to have anything to do with them. Organised religion is so caught up in its own rites and regulations that it has lost its direction totally, light years away from its original brief.

The concept of something after death does not just puzzle the will, it also creates a challenge as to how mere humans might convincingly describe it or even glimpse a shadow of something after death. Words, I have decided, especially religious ones, cannot do it. They are too precise, too mundane, too bound up with the practicalities of life on earth. Even Shakespeare avoids anything more than vague comments on a divinity that shapes our ends and balks at any attempt to define it or bring us a description of it, rough-hewn or not.

However, I am loath to give up on the quest for the undiscovered country, for some indication that our lives are not just ant-like nonentities in a purely Darwinian order. If any form of communication can express the inexpressible it is music. Here we are not bound by the precision of dictionary definitions but are involved in an international language, expressing all those emotional and conceptual matters that words fail to convey: joy, sorrow, anguish, love, hatred, peace and even a little bit more.

So, I would not turn to poetry or popes for solace or enlightenment. I would go to Bach, or Mozart, or Beethoven (at times) or Schubert. These people have the gift to intimate that there is something more to the human spirit than the 9 o'clock news or Drumcree church. Because these great composers are free of verbal restrictions they can let their imagination fly and take us at least part of the way with them. At their finest they can suggest that they have been privileged to a preview of something beyond us ordinary folk's ken and they provide us with a glimpse of it, too, through the very special power of communication called music.

Poetry has served music well, providing it with textual references, with inspirational moments. A diminutive, podgy, young, hard-drinking, party-going lad in Vienna some 170 years ago had an exceptional gift for putting words and music together better to serve both. However, though Franz Schubert may have been the most sublime of all composers, he was not always the best judge of good verse. He set some terrible dross, though it belonged to the highly popular genre of 'bleeding hearts' and unrequited love then in vogue. Sometimes he set worthy texts, including Shakespeare and Goethe, but he also enhanced the words of less well-known writers, whose names would remain in academic archives if it had not been for the shaft of music light with which he illuminated their endeavours.

Most important of these is a tiny 8-line mini-poem by Franz von Schober. He was one of the wild Schubertian bunch that partied until they dropped, though after Schubert's early death he went to Hungary and became Liszt's secretary for a time. He did not marry until he was 60, to a lady who edited magazines for teenage girls. Unfortunately he never wrote a proper memoir of his time with Schubert, without whom his name would be scarcely remembered today.

Schubert turned his friend's little poem into one of the most sublime utterances in all of music. The tune is embarrassingly simple, yet he conjured a feeling of infinite possibilities, of worlds beyond our understanding, in a few brief pages of music. We may not be able to enjoy the sound just now but we can savour Schober's octave, while echoes of Schubert's melody steal into our inner ear that is the bliss of solitude. Half a loaf, after all...

Yours sincerely

Ian Fox

An die Musik

Du holde Kunst, in wieviel grauen Stunden,
Wo mich des Lebens wilder Kries umstrickt
Hast du mein Herz zu warmer Lieb entzunden,
Hast mich in eine bessre Welt entrückt!

Oft hat ein Seufzer, deiner Harf entflossen,
Ein süsser, heiliger Akkord von dir
Den Himmel bessrer Zeiten mir erschlossen,
Du holde Kunst, ich danke dir dafür!

FRANZ VON SCHOBER (1796–1882)

To Music

You gracious art, in many grey hours
When I have been caught up in life's turbulence
You have kindled a warm love in my heart
Transporting me into a better world!

Oft has a sigh, flowing from your harp,
One of your sweet divine chords
Opened up the heaven of better times,
You gracious art, I thank you for that!

ITA DALY

Dear Marie Heaney

I am sorry to take so long to reply to your letter but I have been struggling with the word spiritual – a word which has always given me problems. I always think that it has religious connotations, a hang-over for those of us who have left conventional religion behind but are still not ready to accept the gloom of extinction. In other words, I think there can be a dishonest concept behind the word.

Having said that, when I have felt close to despair the world of nature has supplied a sort of leavening, particularly a stretch of countryside beyond Bangor Erris in County Mayo where the land stretches forever and the horizon keeps receding as you walk. Something about the immensity of the landscape helps one gain a perspective. Is this spiritual sustenance?

Sincerely
Ita Daly

BERNARD FARRELL

Dear Marie

Many thanks for inviting me to contribute my personal choice of spiritual sustenance. Heavens above – where to start? (Or vice-versa.)

Poetry, of course, has always been a rich source – but also the prose of Hesse, Thoreau, Wolfe and Salinger and (in more desperate times!) Joyce, Greene and Mailer. Often, the choices have had to be rapidly abandoned (as my needs changed) – but always, and to this day, there has been the constant wisdom and humanity of John Steinbeck.

Some years ago, I visited Monterey, the setting of his wonderfully uplifting novel, Cannery Row. *I was there more as a pilgrim than as a traveller – for this was my Lourdes, my Mecca, my Moscow.*

Two short examples should hopefully reflect his gift. Both feature the street-philosopher, Doc, as he observes 'Mack and the boys', regarded by all as the down-and-outs, the dregs of society, the flotsam and jetsam of Cannery Row.

> Doc said, 'Look at them. There are your true philosophers. I think,' he went on, 'that Mack and the boys know everything that has ever happened in the world and possibly everything that will happen. I think they survive in this particular world better than other people. In a time when people tear themselves to pieces with ambition and nervousness and covetousness, they are relaxed. All of our so-called successful men are sick men, with bad stomachs, and bad souls, but Mack and the boys are healthy and curiously clean. They can do what they want. They can satisfy their appetites without calling them something else.'

And later, Steinbeck allows Doc to sum up thus:

> 'It has always seemed strange to me,' said Doc. 'The things we admire in men – kindness and generosity, openness, honesty, understanding and feeling – are

the concomitants of failure in our system. And those traits we detest – sharpness, greed, acquisitiveness, meanness, egotism and self-interest – are the traits of success. And while men admire the quality of the first, they love the produce of the second.'

With very best wishes
Bernard Farrell

GARY HASTINGS

Dear Marie

I have come across this story below in a number of places. I have no idea of its origins. It is a simple story on the face of it, but the epigram on the ring has had great depth for me in reflection. The idea that transience, change itself, can be both a constant and a comfort as well as a disturbance, provoking newness and rethinking, is a continual, self-renewing surprise for me. This is more than simply, 'There's a good time coming,' on the one hand and 'Temperance in all things,' on the other – it is possible to seek the nature of the divine in the continuity of change itself.

It ties in too with the Christian ideas of death as possibility – healing and cure, rest and fulfilment; beginning, not end and failure.

One image we have of eternity is stasis, unending, unchanging. But perhaps new life in Christ should bring the understanding to cope with, ride out and live through the changes which are life itself. Eternal life is not eternal death, for only death is free of change, only the 'not alive' remains nearly the same. God as creative, God as life, God underpinning existence might not actually be, in one sense, the 'eternal changelessness' of the prayer Anglicans are familiar with, but might be that which is the one and only constant in life and existence – change, mutability. Perhaps God is more in that essence than the eternal, immutable, frozen image many find hard to worship, approach or understand.

Once a king commanded that all his craftsmen and wise men be gathered together. He demanded that they should come up with something which when he was sad would make him happy, and when he was happy could make him sad. They all tried, and thought and worked, but only one of them came up with anything. It was a ring, and on it was engraved: 'This too will pass.'

Beir bua agus beannacht
Gary Hastings

RORY BRENNAN

Dear Marie

Many thanks for asking me to contribute to your anthology in aid of Focus Ireland.

The word spiritual is a tarnished one for me. I belong to that last generation to be educated by the Catholic Church in Ireland when a pitiless mediaeval wind still blew through the classroom, combining the inky orthodoxy of the scriptorium with a whiff of a dank dungeon. We were 'schoolmen' in a philosophical sense as well, though indeed we did not know it.

The word 'spiritual' meant devotional. Your 'spiritual life' meant observation of sacramental obligations and the avoidance of certain 'sins'.

The word moral is similarly diminished for me. So, like a great many, I have had to re-invent meanings and terms. I should like to make a distinction between the spirit and the spiritual. The concept of spirit I take as devoid of cloudy religious trappings inherent in the spiritual. The spirit stands for courage, original thought, political liberty, resilience, and is closely connected to what is meant by the heart and the capacity to love.

From adolescence courage has seemed to me the most important of the virtues, for without it love is frail and charity is crippled. Works of art which encourage – directly give strength to – the spirit have always appealed to me. Paul Valéry's line 'Le vent se lève!… Il faut tenter de vivre!' ('The wind is stirring… We must try to live') carried with it (in French) that sense of the indomitable which I have always found to be a source of solace and resolution. The poem by Louis MacNeice below, the last one he wrote, mixes a rugged worldliness with a commitment to the spirit's bruising, but ever-enticing quest, first for joy and then for understanding.

All best wishes
Rory Brennan

Thalassa

Run out the boat, my broken comrades;
Let the old seaweed crack, the surge
Burgeon oblivious of the last
Embarkation of feckless men,
Let every adverse force converge –
Here we must needs embark again.

Run up the sail, my heartsick comrades;
Let each horizon tilt and lurch –
You know the worst: your wills are fickle,
Your values blurred, your hearts impure
And your past life a ruined church –
But let your poison be your cure.

Put out to sea, ignoble comrades,
Whose record shall be noble yet;
Butting through scarps of moving marble
The narwhal dares us to be free;
By a high star our course is set,
Our end is Life. Put out to sea.

Louis MacNeice (1907–63)

LOUIS MARCUS

Dear Marie

I wish I could offer some uplifting quotation from sacred writing, or even from (supposedly) secular poetry or prose.

But there is such a discrepancy between high-sounding words and brutal reality that these passages leave me dubious rather than elevated.

Where I find anything resembling spiritual sustenance is in music, more particularly chamber music. Haydn's Op. 20, No. 4 quartet, Mozart's Dissonance *quartet and string quintet in G minor, the* Heiliger Dankgesang *movement from Beethoven's Op. 132 quartet, the Brahms 2nd quartet, the Schubert quintet in C... to mention only a handful.*

Some of this music is dark, if not bleak. But it does suggest, rightly or wrongly, that there may be meaning after all.

Yours sincerely

Louis Marcus

MARY KENNY

Dear Marie

Spirituality is universal, but it is also personal. One size does not fit all.

And perhaps, as with clothes, you only learn what suits you by trying on different items. As with apparel, when you have found your style, stick with it and employ it with confidence.

Soppy spirituality is not my bag. Sermons whose message is 'All you need is love' cause me to roll my eyes. We all need love, but give me other values too: something challenging. The fascination of what's difficult. Give me high, exacting standards. Throw in some bracing austerity. Let me have men about me that are robust. (Don't change that to 'people': the allusion is Shakespeare, with which you do not muck around…)

No spiritual book has ever sustained me better than Thomas à Kempis's The Imitation of Christ. *I turn to it again and again. I have worn out two editions over the years. You can't beat the fourteenth century when it comes to high standards, bracing austerity and a demanding challenge.*

Thomas's admonitions are against the world, the flesh and the devil. He abjures all earthly vanities and baubles. He cautions against the pride of knowledge without the humility of holiness. 'Vanity of vanities, and all is vanity,' is a phrase from the Book of Ecclesiastes that clearly thrills him. 'It is vanity to seek riches which must perish, and to trust in them. It is vanity also to be ambitious of honours, and to raise oneself to a high station. It is vanity to follow the desires of the flesh… It is vanity to wish for a long life, and to take little care of leading a good life.'

In the age of the Internet and the clamour of information technology, I find some of his observations most prescient. 'Cast aside that excessive desire for knowledge; because much distraction is found there and much delusion… There are many things the knowledge of which is of little or no profit to the soul.'

Thomas, a German monk who lived to be 93 years old, was a

fountain of wisdom. 'All perfections in this life are attended with some imperfection, and all our speculations with a certain obscurity.' He is keen on the pursuit of virtue, which I find inspiring, and of the crushing of vice, which I find usefully testing. Learning in itself does not make people virtuous. 'Learning is not to be condemned… but a good conscience and a virtuous life are always to be preferred. But because many strive after knowledge rather than to live well, therefore they are often deceived, and bring forth little or no fruit.' Many vicious people – look at the Nazis and all their science – have been highly knowledgeable.

He warns against gullibility, which, again, in the age of spin-doctors and mass advertising, strikes me as highly relevant. 'We must not believe every word we hear nor follow every impulse; but carefully and prudently weigh the matter according to God.' (In spite of my experience of life, I can be surprisingly gullible about some things. Adverts for cosmetics which mendaciously proclaim that they 'halt the ageing process' instantly convince me, I notice. Talk about vanity of vanities.)

He can be very, very austere. He disapproves of all idle chatter and pointless prattle. There is far too much partying for Thomas's liking: Pascal's reflection, two centuries later, that most human mischief derives from the fact that we cannot sit quietly in a room alone, must derive from Thomas à Kempis.

Thomas is chillingly frank about impending death. 'A very little while and all will be over with you here; consider then how matters stand with you; a man is here today, and tomorrow he is gone… You ought, in every action and thought, to regulate yourself as if you were to die immediately.' Bracing. But did not Yeats say something similar: 'From our birthday until we die/Is but the twinkling of an eye'?

And yet, for all his tough talk I find Thomas à Kempis consoling. He brings me down to earth, and at the same time, he uplifts my spirit. Especially when I am feeling low, interestingly. You don't want prattle when you are depressed: you want someone to take you seriously.

He provides a kind of contrasting balm to the hubbub of modern life, which heaven knows is full of pointless prattle and empty talk. Journalism, which is my profession, also has a frustratingly shallow side. It is all here today and gone tomorrow and one is left with no sense of the eternal. One needs the counterpoint of his profondeurs.

His words are intensely consoling in terms of personal disappointment. I am, in all probability, in the third quarter of my earthly life now (for all I know, indeed, the last quarter), and in many spheres I am disappointed with myself. Who isn't? But I thought I would achieve more. I thought I would be cleverer than I am. I thought I would do great things. But I have turned out to be rather a mediocrity, and I shall die without attaining any of the glittering prizes to which I aspired.

This is when Thomas à Kempis proves such a tonic. Detach yourself from earthly things, he intones. Cease to indulge yourself in vanities and self-regard. 'The reason why so many things displease and often disturb you, is that you are not as yet perfectly dead to yourself, nor detached from earthly things… Never think you have made any progress until you consider yourself to be inferior to all.' Don't even think of getting yourself those glittering prizes…

A friend of mine who resides in Japan has found in Shinto Buddhism some of the same values as Thomas à Kempis. The four noble truths of Shinto Buddhism are: 1: All Life is Suffering. 2: Suffering is caused by Desire. 3: Desire is focused on the Self. 4: In the elimination of the Self lies the suppression of Desire.

Great minds think alike, eh?

Actually, I'm also fond of a Californian sort-of Buddist-ish text entitled Don't Sweat the Small Stuff. *It's by Richard Carlson, and in style, it couldn't be more different from the* Imitation. *It's real laid-back West Coast stuff; and yet there are hidden similarities.*

> Don't sweat the small stuff. Most things don't matter too much. If someone acts mean to you, or the shop doesn't stock what you yearn for, or the traffic is awfully bad today, don't let it get to you. It's no big deal.

> Some people are not going to like you. Some people are going to criticise you. Some people are always going to disapprove of you. Accept it. Surrender to the fact that life isn't fair.

When vexations arise, ask yourself – 'Will this matter a year from now?' Hey, you won't even remember most of what irks you today a year from now.

Ignore negative thoughts. Perform a random act of kindness. Do someone a secret favour. Be grateful when you're feeling good and graceful when you're feeling bad. Remind yourself that when you die, your 'In' basket won't be empty.

This, too, helps me make it through the night.
Mary Kenny

JOHN B KEANE

Dear Marie

My choice of poem is 'I See You Dancing Father' by Brendan Kennelly. I choose this poem because our fathers when recalled lovingly and sincerely are never dead or forgotten. The love of son for father is the essence of loyalty and devotion. Brendan Kennelly's father comes to life here; so does my own dear, departed dad.

John B Keane

I See You Dancing, Father

No sooner downstairs after the night's rest
And in the door
Than you started to dance a step
In the middle of the kitchen floor.

And as you danced
You whistled.
You made your own music
Always in tune with yourself.

Well, nearly always, anyway.
You're buried now
In Lislaughtin Abbey
And whenever I think of you

I go back beyond the old man
Mind and body broken
To find the unbroken man.
It is the moment before the dance begins,

Your lips are enjoying themselves
Whistling an air.
Whatever happens or cannot happen
In the time I have to spare
I see you dancing, father.

BRENDAN KENNELLY (1936–)

CAROLINE WALSH

Dear Marie

Many thanks for your letter. When I tried to decide on a text or a piece of music or song that always uplifts me, the one that beat all possibilities into first place was the poem 'Canal Bank Walk' by Patrick Kavanagh.

I chose it because interwoven into it are two concepts, both a major source of renewal for me; Nature as a healer, and long-term association with place as a perennial fount of regeneration.

From the age of seven until well into my 20s I lived a lot of my life within yards of the Grand Canal in Dublin. I often saw Paddy Kavanagh walking its tow paths on the stretch along Wilton Place leading towards Baggot Street Bridge. Only when I grew up did I understand the power he invested in his canal poems like the one included here and 'Lines Written on a Seat on the Grand Canal, Dublin, "Erected to the Memory of Mrs. Dermot O'Brien"'. Rooted as he was in the soil around Inniskeen, his head full of 'Mullahinsha, Drummeril, Black Shanco –' it was as if while pounding the pavements of Dublin 2, the canal was his conduit back to Monaghan, to the country world where he was 'king of banks and stones and every blooming thing'.

The central idea in 'Canal Bank Walk', that a soul can be remade again by walking leafy banks, by watching a bird gathering twigs for a nest, is utterly convincing to me because I've done it – and it's worked. Many times.

Because the canal poems are redolent of the particular stretch of the canal I walked day in day out in the sixties, going to school in Miss Meredith's, they have helped invest that small part of Dublin with something very strong for me. Sometimes, stretched from the cut and thrust of what's become a very fast world – and an utterly changed city – I decide to walk home from work, cutting across Fitzwilliam Square and Lad Lane through to the canal, the small patch where I grew up with my mother and sisters, surrounded by the other families who also once lived there. And there is a great power attached to the memory of that world. It's as though all those people are a chorus there still, somehow forcefully urging me on.

The other place that has the same effect are the fields, river banks and old demesne avenues around Bective in County Meath where I also spent much of my childhood. For that reason there are many passages in the work of Meath writers like Mary Lavin and Lord Dunsany and the poet Francis Ledwidge which, apart from being great in their own right, have that same regenerative power for me because I know those same lanes and hills and the little villages dotting the landscape. Their texts become the scripts of a personalised genus loci that are both a history of a personal past and a map towards a future. Tribal ancestors trod here. They can't be let down.

I don't 'have' either of these places any more in the sense that my family no longer lives in them but they stay with me and through the writers who have immortalised aspects of them I feel I will never lose them.

That's why I am so glad the royalties from your book are going to Focus Ireland and the homeless. To me to be separated from the places along the way one calls home or – unthinkably worse – never to have inherited the gift of a love of home or an identification with a particular place would be fate at its most impoverished.

Once again many thanks for asking me to contribute to your project.

Caroline Walsh

Canal Bank Walk

Leafy-with-love banks and the green waters of the canal
Pouring redemption for me, that I do
The will of God, wallow in the habitual, the banal,
Grow with nature again as before I grew.
The bright stick trapped, the breeze adding a third
Party to the couple kissing on an old seat,
And a bird gathering materials for the nest for the Word
Eloquently new and abandoned to its delirious beat.
O unworn world enrapture me, enrapture me in a web
Of fabulous grass and eternal voices by a beech,
Feed the gaping need of my senses, give me ad lib
To pray unselfconsciously with overflowing speech
For this soul needs to be honoured with a new dress woven
From green and blue things and arguments that cannot be
proven.

PATRICK KAVANAGH (1904–67)

STANISLAUS KENNEDY

In the beginning was the word
The word was with God
And the word was God.
He was with God in the beginning
Through him all things came to be,
Not one thing had its being but through him.

(FROM PROLOGUE TO ST JOHN'S GOSPEL)

Dear Marie

Thank you for your invitation to contribute to your book about what it is that influences and sustains my spiritual life. What a big question! As well as time alone in prayer and in reflection and time with people and with nature there are many poems and writings and pieces of scripture that I draw on for sustenance every day, and I keep finding new ones. I cannot possibly nominate one particular piece, and so, if you will allow me, I will mention a few, though I could name dozens and dozens!

First let me explain my understanding of spirituality. I do not see it, as I think some people do, as withdrawal, turning inward to attend to God and one's inner self. My understanding of spirituality is quite different. It assumes a way of being in the world that demands an even deeper involvement and immersion in the world than is usual and it is underpinned by the conviction that everything that is, is holy (although not yet completely so).

In Genesis 2, God breathes into the dust of the earth in order to create us human beings. Thus we are made of a mixture of breath (the divine) and dust (the earthly), and, as the poet Wendell Berry puts it, 'the dustier and breathier we are, the better'. It is our job as human beings to keep those two sources, dust and breath, together, and that is holy work.

The way we draw dust and breath together is by seeing God in everything, and everything in God, and that is how I understand the spiritual life. Kavanagh, in his poem 'Ploughman', expresses this for me:

Ploughman

I turn the lea-green down
Gaily now,
And paint the meadow brown
With my plough.

I dream with silvery gull
And brazen crow,
A thing that is beautiful
I may know.

Tranquillity walks with me
And no care.
O, the quiet ecstasy
Like a prayer.

I find a star-lovely art
In a dark sod.
Joy that is timeless! O heart
That knows God!

PATRICK KAVANAGH (1904–67)

A similar sentiment is expressed in this extract from a poem from a very different tradition, Songs of Kabir *(by the poet Kabir of the fourteenth/fifteenth century, translated by Rabindranath Tagore, in the nineteenth century):*

Within this earthen vessel are bowers and groves, and
within it is the Creator:
Within this vessel are the seven oceans and the
unnumbered stars.
The touchstone and the jewel-appraiser are within:
And within this vessel the Eternal soundeth, and the
spring wells up.
Kabir says: 'Listen to me, my Friend! My beloved Lord
is within.'

KABIR (14TH / 15TH CENTURY)

For me, the way to live the spiritual life, to perceive the divine in the everyday, is to live in a spirit of joyful gratitude, to realise that everything is gift. The psalms, many of them, are great songs of praise and gratitude, but for me, the greatest song of gratitude in the bible is the Canticle of Daniel:

Canticle of Daniel

All things the Lord has made, bless the Lord:
give glory and eternal praise to him...

Sun and moon! bless the Lord:
give glory and eternal praise to him.
Stars of heaven! bless the Lord:
give glory and eternal praise to him.
Winds! all bless the Lord:
give glory and eternal praise to him.
Fire and heat! Bless the Lord:
give glory and eternal praise to him.
Cold and heat! Bless the Lord:
give glory and eternal praise to him.
Dews and sleets! Bless the Lord
give glory and eternal praise to him.
Frost and cold! bless the Lord:
give glory and eternal praise to him.
Ice and snow! bless the Lord:
give glory and eternal praise to him.
Nights and days! bless the Lord:
give glory and eternal praise to him.
Light and darkness! bless the Lord:
give glory and eternal praise to him.
Lightning and clouds! bless the Lord:
give glory and eternal praise to him.
Let the earth bless the Lord:
give glory and eternal praise to him.
Mountains and hills! bless the Lord:
give glory and eternal praise to him.
Everything that grows on the earth! bless the Lord:
give glory and eternal praise to him.
Springs of water! bless the Lord:
give glory and eternal praise to him.
Seas and rivers! bless the Lord:
give glory and eternal praise to him.
Sea beasts and everything that lives in water! bless the Lord:
give glory and eternal praise to him.
Birds of heaven! bless the Lord:
give glory and eternal praise to him.

Animals wild and tame! bless the Lord:
give glory and eternal praise to him.
For he has snatched us from the underworld
saved us from the hand of death,
saved us from the burning fiery furnace,
rescued us from the heart of the flame.
Give thanks to the Lord, for he is good,
for his love is everlasting.
All you who worship him, bless the God of gods,
praise him and give him thanks,
for his love is everlasting.

*I used to think that we are grateful to God because we are happy;
now I realise that we are happy because we are grateful. True joy and
happiness comes from a wholehearted response to whatever
opportunity is given to me at any moment no matter how difficult.
This poem of Denise Levertov's expresses what I mean:*

Each day's terror
almost a form of boredom – madmen
at the wheel and
stepping on the gas and
the brakes no good –
and each day one,
sometimes two, morning glories,
faultless, blue, blue sometimes
flecked with magenta, each
lit from within with
the first sunlight.

DENISE LEVERTOV (1923–)

*Levertov is here expressing what we might think of as the spirituality
of the commuter, beginning by describing the horrors of driving to
work every morning, and then shifting suddenly to savour the
beauty that morning also brings.*

*I am a morning person myself, and I try to begin each day with a
walk at dawn or shortly afterwards, and to take the opportunity to be
grateful for the morning and for the coming day. The world is reborn
every morning and we are given a whole new time and opportunity
each day. The sunrise is a reminder of each day's gift because it comes
involuntarily. We don't and cannot produce it.*

It is poetry that has taught me how to be surprised at the world. As long as we go around unsurprised, taking things for granted, we never see the light and reality remains opaque. The opposite of taking things for granted is a willingness to be constantly surprised: to the extent to which we allow surprise to flow into our lives, to that extent our whole lives become translucent with gratefulness, as we allow surprise to grow into gracefulness.

Near the end of his letter to the Philippians (4: 4-7), St Paul urges Christians to be happy, joyful and grateful. I read this as an expansion on what Jesus meant when he said 'You are the light of the world.' This is often understood to be about telling others about doctrine, but I think that is too limited an understanding of this text. To me it means, 'Listen! This is a dark world. If you shine your light it will make the world a little brighter. So shine, be happy, be joyful, be grateful and you will light up the life of others.'

We arrive at an ability to be surprised, to be grateful and to be joyful by taking the time to see God in all things, by taking time to read, to reflect and above all to be alone and still within ourselves, and to allow the presence of God to flow through us. If we could be still with God we would be able to give away that presence to all Life:

from Duino Elegies

Oh, if for once all were completely still!
If all mere happenstance and chance
were silenced, and the laughter next door, too;
if all that droning of my senses
did not prevent my being wide awake –
Then, with one thousandfold thought,
I would reach your horizon
and, for the span of a smile, hold you
to give you away to all life
as thanksgiving.

RAINER MARIA RILKE (1875–1926)

With the artists, poets, writers, I have learned the importance of taking time alone and in stillness, getting out of my own way, pushing beyond the enclosure of my human ego and into the lively world of the other. It is in silence and stillness that I come to see God in the hearts and minds and bodies of the silent ones, poor and fragile people, and it is in silence and stillness that God speaks to me through the wisdom that comes from them. This is what I believe Jesus meant when he said 'In so far as you do it to the least of my brothers and sisters, you do it to me.'

Wishing you all the very best with the project.

God bless

Sr Stanislaus Kennedy

'Spirituality is universal, but it is also personal. One size does not fit all and perhaps, as with clothes, you only learn what suits you by trying on different items.'

Mary Kenny

'I used to think that we are grateful to God because we are happy; now I realise that we are happy because we are grateful.'

Sr Stanislaus Kennedy

'Though I am not a Christian, I identify strongly with this urge to worship, and to be transported by, the experience of the natural world.'

Paula Meehan

'When my mother was ill, I came on her one day half asleep, the cat half asleep on her lap. The afternoon sun shone on them both. My mother had done nothing. Neither had the cat. Yet between them, they had created a moment of perfection, of total acceptance. This, too, was an achievement.'

Olivia O'Leary

'In a lifetime of gratitude and regrets one
of the most serious regrets is the repeated
hesitancy on the edge of silence, on the
threshold of contemplation.'

Professor Enda McDonagh

'The sequence of primes is an endless seam
of stitches joining reason to the
incomprehensible.'

Tim Robinson

'No one makes the kind of sense
that Christ makes... no one matters to me
more.'

Desmond Egan

'Doris Lessing calls coincidences God's
way of remaining anonymous.'

Mark Patrick Hederman

MAUREEN CAIRNDUFF

Dear Marie

Multiplication tables by rote defeated me then and now. Yet I can clearly remember prayers and poems. 'Hail Holy Queen' is one of the saddest prayers invented. The 'Our Father' covers the ground well but is a bit mundane. The Rosary – too long. The 'Act of Contrition' is an essential part of travel, to be recited with lips moving on take off and landing. It is not that I lack confidence in the pilot, really it is superstition, fear of what might happen if it was not said. Other than those set prayers, communication with God is more direct. Perhaps a good fundamentalist religion might have suited me better. Mass has been discarded due to irritation with the celebrant, letting the singer get in the way of the song.

Communication with the almighty usually takes the form of bargaining, 'If my son gets his exam', 'If I can find my car keys', 'If the traffic lets me get to the airport on time', 'If it turns out to be benign' – then I'll be good tempered and charitable all day, even all week, it never extends beyond seven days. Never promise what you cannot deliver. Sometimes God listens and sometimes he doesn't. I never abuse him for negligence and always thank him when he helps out. Even the most trivial thoughtfulness on his part is received with gratitude – just before banging the front door you realise the keys are sitting inside. 'That was a close one, thanks a lot God' or 'I've finally written this piece, thank God.'

Maureen Cairnduff

MARIE-LOUISE O'DONNELL

Dear Marie

Thank you very much for thinking of me. I include my choice of material and my own personal comments.

I wish you a lot of success with the book, which is a brilliant idea. Focus Ireland is a great organisation and I feel privileged to be able to help.

I love this poem.

It's about survival. It's about a spirit in people that can never be quenched.

I always feel that there is God here between the lines, telling me to keep going, despite the odds.

It gives me courage when I can't find any. But most of all it takes away big fears that lurk around corners and won't go away.

I'm afraid of things unknown, but the Caged Bird is joyous and reverential about them, and I know that when he opens his throat to sing, the very purest, clearest and newest sound comes out.

If I met God, I know he'd be able to sing, I'd sing a duet with him that would last all day.

Yours sincerely
Marie-Louise O'Donnell

Caged Bird

A free bird leaps
on the back of the wind
and floats downstream
till the current ends
and dips his wing
in the orange sun rays
and dares to claim the sky.

But a bird that stalks
down his narrow cage
can seldom see through
his bars of rage
his wings are clipped and
his feet are tied
so he opens his throat to sing.

The caged bird sings
with a fearful trill
of things unknown
but longed for still
and his tune is heard
on the distant hill
for the caged bird
sings of freedom.

The free bird thinks of another breeze
and the trade winds soft through the sighing trees
and the fat worms waiting on a dawn-bright lawn
and he names the sky his own.

But a caged bird stands on the grave of dreams
his shadow shouts on a nightmare scream
his wings are clipped and his feet are tied
so he opens his throat to sing.

The caged bird sings
with a fearful trill
of things unknown
but longed for still
and his tune is heard
on the distant hill
for the caged bird
sings of freedom.

MAYA ANGELOU (1928–)

PETER SOMERVILLE-LARGE

Dear Marie Heaney

I am delighted to be invited to contribute to your book on ideas of spiritual sustenance and to support Focus Ireland.

I came from a family that had its share of travellers, soldiers and servants of Empire. Our house was full of heads of wild animals, carved teak tables, planter's chairs, a set of Japanese ivory figures depicting torture scenes and cannon-balls picked up after the siege of Sevastopol and converted into inkwells. Perhaps that is partly the reason why I have always been obsessed by the idea of the exploration of unknown and distant places.

As a boy I read travel books obsessively, particularly books about Central Asia such as Sven Hedin's Central Asia and Tibet, *Auriel Stein's* Sand-buried Ruins of Khotan, *Colonel Schomberg's* Peaks and Plains of Central Asia. *I read the memoirs of Curzon, Durand, and Colonel Younghusband who was entertained in the high snows of the Pamirs by a group of Russian officers, and toasted the Queen and the Czar in champagne. I planned to follow in the footsteps of these men and visit Kashgar, the Wakhan, the Pamirs and the Turkoman desert.*

In the nineteen-fifties the Oxus was still far distant, the Karakoram Highway was not yet a monstrous plan for opening up Central Asia, frontiers had not closed and countries that have since been devastated by savage wars had a measure of civilisation that was not yet destroyed. It is impossible nowadays to recreate the magic and promise of travel that still existed in those far-off days.

I did not fulfil my ambitions and have remained a frustrated nomad. (I have moved house over twenty times.) But I was fortunate enough to see many places in a time of innocence before the jet plane, the Kalashnikov and tourism conquered the world. I travelled in Afghanistan, Nepal and Borneo with a sense of discovery and exhilaration that could not be reproduced today. In the early eighties I crossed Tibet with great difficulty to the holy mountain of Kailash and the sacred lake of Mansoravar which has been called the Navel of the World. Today this journey has become a commonplace of tourism.

Wilfred Thesiger achieved what I only dreamed about in his exploration of the secret and distant places of Asia. I find it difficult not to share his disillusion brought about by change and progress. We are too old to take interest in the new frontiers of exploration in space and science. However, the old visions and memories still retain much of their magic and the concept of romantic travel gives me a spiritual dimension which continues to sustain me.

I am a disciple of Thesiger. Here are some of his thoughts on exploration.

Yours sincerely

Peter Somerville-Large

from Arabian Sands

All my life I had hated machines. I could remember how bitterly at school I had resented reading the news that someone had flown across the Atlantic or travelled through the Sahara in a car. I had realised even then that the speed and ease of mechanical transport must rob the world of all diversity...

Everyone knew that there was nothing to be found on the top of Everest, but even in this materialistic age few people asked, 'What point is there in climbing Everest? What good will it do anyone when they are there?' They recognised that even today there are experiences that do not need to be justified in terms of material profit...

No, it is not the goal, but the way there that matters, and the harder the way the more worthwhile the journey. Who, after all, would dispute that it is more satisfying to climb to the top of a mountain than to go there in a funicular railway? Perhaps this was one reason why I resented modern inventions; they made the road too easy. I felt instinctively that it is better to fail on Everest without oxygen than to attain the summit with its use. If climbers used oxygen, why should they not have their supplies dropped to them from aeroplanes, or landed by helicopter? Yet to refuse mechanical aids as unsporting reduced exploration to the level of a sport like big-game shooting in Kenya when the hunter is allowed to drive up to

within sight of the animal but must get out of the car to shoot
it. I would not myself have wished to cross the Empty
Quarter in a car. Luckily this was impossible when I did my
journeys, for to have done the journey on a camel when I
could have done it in a car would have turned the venture
into a stunt.

WILFRED THESIGER

ROBIN EAMES

> Seeing then that we have been entrusted with this
> commission, which we owe entirely to God's mercy, we
> never lose heart.

2 CORINTHIANS 1

Dear Editor

*I find this verse a mixture of reassurance, strength and spiritual
encouragement. At times it is all too easy to lose heart and to become
discouraged. As a Church leader in Ireland through many years of
suffering and heartache for many people I have met many whose faith
in God has been tested by their experiences. Leadership is taxing and
costly. At times misunderstanding and opposition are powerful but
negative forces. To seek to do the will of God is not an easy option. It
leads to its own testing and challenge on an individual basis. These
words from St Paul have given me encouragement in many a dark
moment. The call to serve God and through him to serve people is a
commission of no little value. It is through his mercy alone that we
respond to such a call. Who then are we to lose heart when given
such a task to complete? In a spiritual sense God's presence and love
is sufficient for all our needs as we respond to whatever task he gives
us.*

✠ Robert, Armagh

EUGENE McCABE

Dear Marie

It was Sunday when Paddy (20) phoned and asked:

'What's it like at home now... the weather?'

'Raining,' I said.

'Raining here too in Manhattan.'

And we talked on. Near the end of the call he said:

'I've been looking down at the street all morning thinking about Drumard, going round and round every field in my head, I can see them all as clear as anything.'

After that image of grieving it was hard to keep talking.

And it was Margot's cousin, Michael O'Grady (40 years in Arizona), who inherited his widowed mother's house in a village in County Clare. Sometimes, he said, he'd dial the number from Phoenix just to hear the phone ringing three thousand miles away, in that empty room in Kildysart.

Two images that could be added to by almost every family in the country and partly why I find this translation of 'Columcille's Farewell' so moving. It's not only the pervasive sense of death. The voice is full of passionate heartbreak as he calls out to his beloved people and places, to Ireland itself. Are there two sadder lines in any language than the closing couplet? If there are I have yet to come across them.

Every wish

Eugene McCabe

Columcille's Farewell

How quickly my coracle speeds on,
The salt spray blinds my gaze,
I grieve on the trackless sea,
Sailing from Ireland to Alba of the Ravens.

The Cliffs grow small,
As through a mist of death my eyes look back,
I shall never see again,
The wives of Ireland or their men.

Gael, Gael, oh precious name,
Broken is my heart within my breast,
Should sudden death overtake me,
It is for my great love of the Gael.

Beloved are Durrow and Derry,
Beloved is Raphoe in purity,
Beloved Drumhone of rich fruits,
Beloved are Swords and Kells.

Beloved to my heart is the West,
Drumcliff and Culcinne Strand,
Their salt mains on which seagulls cry,
The bareness of their rocks and shores.

How cruelly my coracle speeds on,
Wrenching from my gaze the earth I love.
Oh God the bitter sea is teeming on my face,
Sailing from Ireland to Alba of the Ravens.

AUTHOR UNKNOWN

SEAMUS HEANEY

Dear Marie

'Spiritual sustenance', meaning whatever sustains the spirit, supports it from below, maintains its vitality and reinforces its sense of its own validity... Different from what might be called 'spiritual transport', from the catch in the breath, the invitation to ecstasy that can happen when you let up a blind on a May morning or watch a brilliant juggler. What sustains is more returnable to, less surprising, less intense, more tried and chosen. In fact, it can sometimes seem that your sustenance ends up choosing you rather than the other way around.

Why, for example, out of all the bits and pieces you get to know by heart in the course of a lifetime, why do certain quotations keep recurring to you? Or perhaps the question should be, why do you recur to them, since spiritual sustenance involves that feeling of a perfect match between what is needed and what has been supplied. The feeling of a gap closing and at the same time, equally and paradoxically, of a space opening. It seems at those moments that we are made for illumination. Something that we needed to be sure of is entering us and yet it also feels as if it is being located somewhere deep inside us.

The longer I live, the more sustenance I get from William Blake's poem 'Auguries of Innocence'. This is a great litany of insight and outrage, a Romantic poet's supplement to the scriptures, a kind of Sermon on the Thames spoken by a visionary who was also a revolutionary, a man who (in WB Yeats's marvellous statement of the case) 'beat upon the wall/Till truth obeyed his call.' In every couplet of the poem, you feel that a limit is being pushed even as a centre is being reached. The rhymes have a nursery clarity and cogency, the statements have a vivid, one-off here-and-nowness about them, and yet an element of strangeness remains. The truths being told are more like those enshrined in Zen koans than those on the mottoes in fortune cookies, but for all their obliquity, they go straight to the heart of personal and public reality. What makes each and every one of these couplets a separate, two-line truth-capsule is the combination of great simplicity, great intellectual concentration

*and great imaginative sweep. I have my own little Pentecost every
time I say:*

> The wild deer, wand'ring here and there,
> Keeps the Human Soul from Care.

*Just repeating the words wakens a readiness. You have been to the
mountain and back in a flash. No matter how stale you may be
feeling, you are brought to your senses, reminded all over again of
what it was like to be limber in body and mind. You are sustained.
And that's only one couplet out of sixty-six.*

*Like the Sermon on the Mount, 'Auguries of Innocence' calls you
towards the horizon of your understanding and your moral
obligation. It doesn't hector, it takes you back to a time when you had
a more aggravated sense of injustice and a more pristine sense of
spiritual challenge. To read it is to go for a wade in the river of life. It
is not otherworldly. In fact, it is deeply and originally political in
that it understands how everything in life is linked, how cowardice
in the soul issues in corruption in the state, how a failure of nerve in
the bystander is ultimately responsible for callousness in the culture.
But the main thing about it is that it is poetry, something you blink
awake to and yet seem to be witnessing as if it were being dreamt.*

Seamus

Auguries of Innocence

To see a World in a Grain of Sand
And a Heaven in a Wild Flower,
Hold Infinity in the palm of your hand
And Eternity in an hour.

A Robin Redbreast in a Cage
Puts all Heaven in a Rage.
A dove house fill'd with doves and pigeons
Shudders Hell thro' all it regions.
A dog starv'd at his Master's Gate
Predicts the ruin of the State.
A Horse misus'd upon the Road
Calls to Heaven for Human blood.
Each outcry of the hunted Hare
A fibre from the Brain does tear.

A Skylark wounded in the wing
A Cherubim does cease to sing.
The Game Cock clip'd and arm'd for fight
Does the Rising Sun affright.
Every Wolf's and Lion's howl
Raises from Hell a Human Soul.
The wild deer, wand'ring here and there,
Keeps the Human Soul from Care.
The Lamb Misus'd breeds Public strife
And yet forgives the Butcher's Knife.
The Bat that flits at close of Eve
Has left the Brain that won't Believe.
The Owl that calls upon the Night
Speaks the Unbeliever's fright.
He who shall hurt the little Wren
Shall never be belov'd by Men.
He who the Ox to wrath has mov'd
Shall never be by Woman lov'd.
The wanton Boy that kills the Fly
Shall feel the spider's enmity.
He who torments the Chafer's sprite
Weaves a Bower in endless Night.
The Catterpiller on the Leaf
Repeats to thee thy Mother's grief.
Kill not the Moth nor Butterfly,
For the Last Judgement draweth nigh.
He who shall train the Horse to War
Shall never pass the Polar Bar.
The Beggar's Dog and Widow's Cat,
Feed them and thou wilt grow fat.
The Gnat that sings his Summer's song
Poison gets from Slander's tongue.
The poison of the Snake and Newt
Is the sweat of Envy's Foot.
The Poison of the Honey Bee
Is the Artist's Jealousy.
The Prince's Robes and Beggar's Rags
Are Toadstools on the Miser's Bags.
A truth that's told with bad intent
Beats all the Lies you can invent.

It is right it should be so;
Man was made for Joy and Woe;
And when this we rightly know
Thro' the World we safely go,
Joy and Woe are woven fine,
A Clothing for the Soul divine;
Under every grief and pine
Runs a joy with silken twine.
The Babe is more than swaddling Bands;
Throughout all these Human Lands
Tools were made, and Born were hands,
Every Farmer Understands.
Every Tear from Every Eye
Becomes a Babe in Eternity;
This is caught by Females bright
And returns to its own delight.
The Bleat, the Bark, Bellow and Roar
Are Waves that Beat on Heaven's Shore.
The Babe that weeps the Rod beneath
Writes Revenge in realms of death.
The Beggar's Rags, fluttering in Air,
Does to Rags the Heavens tear.
The Soldier, arm'd with Sword and Gun,
Palsied strikes the Summer's Sun.
The poor Man's Farthing is worth more
Than all the Gold on Afric's Shore.
One Mite wrung from the Labrer's hands
Shall buy and sell the Miser's Lands:
Or, if protected from on high,
Does that whole Nation sell and buy.
He who mocks the infant's faith
Shall be mock'd in Age and Death.
He who shall teach the Child to Doubt
The rotting Grave shall ne'er get out.
He who respects the Infant's faith
Triumphs over Hell and Death.
The Child's Toys and the Old Man's Reasons
Are the Fruits of the Two seasons.
The Questioner, who sits so sly,
Shall never know how to Reply.

He who replies to words of Doubt
Doth put the Light of Knowledge out.
The Strongest Poison ever known
Came from Caesar's Laurel Crown.
Nought can deform the Human Race
Like to the Armour's iron brace.
When Gold and Gems adorn the Plow
To peaceful Arts shall Envy Bow.
A Riddle or the Cricket's Cry
Is to Doubt a fit Reply.
The Emmet's Inch and the Eagle's Mile
Make Lame Philosophy to smile.
He who Doubts from what he sees
Will ne'er Believe, do what you Please.
If the Sun and Moon should doubt,
They'd immediately Go out.
To be in a Passion you Good may do,
But no Good if a Passion is in you.
The Whore and Gambler, by the State
Licenc'd, build that Nation's Fate.
The Harlot's cry from Street to Street
Shall weave Old England's winding Sheet.
The Winner's Shout, the Loser's Curse,
Dance before dead England's Hearse.
Every Night and every Morn
Some to Misery are Born.
Every Morn and every Night
Some are Born to sweet delight.
Some are Born to sweet delight,
Some are Born to Endless Night.
We are led to Believe a Lie
When we see not Thro' the Eye
Which was Born in a Night to perish in a Night
When the Soul Slept in Beams of Light.
God Appears and God is Light
To those poor Souls who dwell in Night,
But does a Human Form Display
To those who Dwell in Realms of day.

WILLIAM BLAKE (1757–1827)

NELL McCAFFERTY

Dear Marie

I was approaching the border between Derry and Donegal, cautiously as usual, one spring day before the ceasefire, when I noticed a small bird fly overhead with a huge twig firmly clamped sideways in its beak. It negotiated smooth passage into a tree, despite the awkward cargo, without disturbing a branch. It added the twig to foundations already laid for a nest. I stopped the car and got out to watch. The tree stood between a British army post and an Irish customs post further along. The tree was as busy as Aldergrove airport, with birds flying in and out, bearing twigs. All the birds flew safely home. To all things a season – and then ours came in the North.

Nell McCafferty

MONICA O'CONNOR

Dear Editor

Thank you for inviting me to participate in this project.

The feminist movement has provided me with a wealth of analytical and literary writing from which I draw both strength and solace. Faced as I am every day [at Women's Aid] with the evidence of men's physical and sexual violence against women, it is essential for me to remain connected to both the world-wide movement for women's autonomy and the imaginative freedom created by so many gifted women writers.

The poem I have chosen by the American poet Adrienne Rich expresses for me personal love as a sustaining and inspirational force throughout our lives. It also expresses a recognition of how much is required of our love as we mature: 'Each of us must help the other live/and somewhere, each of us must help the other die.' I especially like the poem's celebration of romance as something that can strike with equal force at any stage of life – we are never too old for love!

Yours faithfully

Monica O'Connor

from Twenty-One Love Poems

III

Since we're not young, weeks have to do time
for years of missing each other. Yet only this odd warp
in time tells me we're not young.
Did I ever walk the morning streets at twenty,
my limbs streaming with a purer joy?
did I lean from any window over the city
listening for the future
as I listen here with nerves tuned for your ring?
And you, you move toward me with the same tempo.

Your eyes are everlasting, the green spark
of the blue-eyed grass of early summer,

the green–blue wild cress washed by the spring.
At twenty, yes: we thought we'd live forever.
At forty-five, I want to know even our limits.
I touch you knowing we weren't born tomorrow,
and somehow, each of us will help the other live,
and somewhere, each of us must help the other die.

ADRIENNE RICH (1929–)

GERALDINE SMYTH

The Coming of Wisdom with Time

Though leaves are many, the root is one;
     Through all the lying days of my youth
I swayed my leaves and flowers in the sun;
     Now I may wither into the truth.

WB YEATS (1865–1939)

Dear Marie

I have carried this poem, like a small nut in my pocket, in the passage from youth to the middle of life. It journeys with me, moved from one coat to another, taken out and held in the hand, something touched and turned around by finger and thumb, connecting me to some kernel of life's final simplicity. At different stages along the way, this short poem has been to me as a nut of wisdom.

The poem itself belongs to a threshold in Yeats's own life when he was still somewhat enthralled by the Celtic Twilight and its blandishments, yet striving to wrest some tougher realism out of the experiences of disappointed love and thwarted ambition. For at another level, it is a poem of coming home to himself as a poet, offering one of those glimpses into the heart's core. The poem looks back on former youthful times, not in nostalgia but with a knowing shake of the head. It implies that what preoccupied the ego then will not satisfy the soul now.

The lazy ease and sway of leaves and flowers in the sun, the pun suggested by the word 'lying' and the carefree laziness of the run-on line, together create a sense of unrelieved self-absorption and self-deception. But, in the last line, a self-critical distance is recovered. There, the abrupt change of diction and rhythm seem to put his new-found wisdom beyond doubt. In this new phase of the journey, in the 'now' of the poem, we see a contrasting picture and mood, with the almost harsh declaration, 'Now I may wither into the truth.'

We respond to the poem's insistence towards truth, not as a flamboyant achievement, but as a grace disclosed in life's gestures of letting go, gestures involving pain, but revealing to us that in the midst of death we are in life. With the insistence that in the end there is but one thing necessary, the frame of the poem closes with the declaration, 'Now I may wither into the truth.'

At different times, I have found myself assenting to the poem's central insight: the journey into wisdom is the path of self-limitation, the letting go of the attachments and distractions of the ego. It is the way of Jesus, the way of the Buddha and of the Sufis. But now in mid-life and standing on the threshold of what writers like Dante have described as the dark wood of life's second journey, I perhaps know and do not know the truth of it, assent to and resist that journey into wisdom, the journey that lies on the other side of darkness. The poem holds the paradox with the concentrated power of a metaphysical conceit – that life is most truly known in dying, fulfilment in being denuded of what we have held dear, that nakedness is the elemental condition of truth.

We recognise Yeats's favoured symbol of the tree as embodying his own desire for 'Unity of Being'. The tree actually embodies the claim of the poem that life in its changing-ness and many-ness is held together and made one, by its hidden underground life. The poem alerts us to the seductions of beauty or success in its many guises and glories. We can concur with the poet's vision of wisdom as a surrender of lush illusion into a barren unconditional place that is inward and downward. We find ourselves drawn into the changing life of the tree with its ancient seasoned wisdom. We experience in the symbol that deep 'Unity of Being' which connects all the pluralities of impulse and imagination, of reason and ideology that divide us from one another, from ourselves and from the truth which is beyond ourselves.

The first and last lines unify the poem, suggesting that in the onward passage from youth to age something holds constant. As we open to this unity of being, we become capable of a new way of seeing. We can read life against the grain of the ego, and against the grain of a culture whose hallmark is an endlessly changing surface of more of the same. Whatever the seeming pattern of change and decay, we glimpse life as deep-down and mysteriously connected and at one with itself.

Reading this poem, thirty years after the first encounter, it still urges me to let go of life's busy fervour and yield to a rhythm that is inward and downward. The poem's four simple lines still evoke the elation and depth that intimate the presence of mystery. But I now notice, for the first time, the self-distrusting hesitation in the last line. There is not here the certainty of life's lesson learned. Rather than the expected resolution of 'I will wither,' we can detect a tone that is more measured – 'Now I may wither into the truth.' I now see here a gentle but necessary reminder of the human frailty that must fringe even our surest wisdom. The poem's parting touch comes as a grace not just to keep us wise, but to keep us humble. In the end, truth reveals itself to us ordinary mortals, in the gap between wisdom and humility.

All good wishes

Geraldine Smyth OP

LELIA DOOLAN

Dear Marie

Many thanks for the invitation to be part of your book for Focus Ireland and Stan and her team and their, hopefully, homebound friends.

There's a lot of spiritual sustenance around. I'd get it as much from the Communist Manifesto as from the Sermon on the Mount – from a good rant about injustice or Beckett's 'I'll go on' as from a good deed in a naughty world.

Belloc has a few lines:

> But they that held through winter to the spring
> Despair as I do and as I do, sing.

or Auden's:

> In bad lands where eggs are small and dear
> Rising to worse by a stonier path when
> All are spent we hear it
> The right song for the wrong time of year.

are to the point.

But these verses by Rilke are glorious and steady things up.

Lelia Doolan

The Swan

This long struggle through the deed still doing
Yet undone that clogs our eager powers,
Imitates the swan's, his way pursuing.
And death, that everlasting, ever-fleeing
From this world on which we stand all hours,
Apes his powerful sloughing of his being.
Sloughed on waters that embrace him gently
And beneath him slide away intently,
Gay at their dismissal, wave on wave;
While through gradual extinction mystic
He, more venerable and more majestic,
Leans to his endeavour, rapt and grave.

RAINER MARIA RILKE (1875–1926)

ÉANNA NÍ LAMHNA

Dear Marie

Thank you for asking me to participate in your proposed book.

Woodlands are spiritual places for me. My earliest memories are of being brought there as a small child by my father to gather sticks and even then being struck by the whole change in atmosphere when we would leave the field and enter the darker woodland with its tall, tall tree trunks.

Now, when walking in them alone my sense of awareness of the surroundings, a sort of spiritual sustenance I suppose, is somehow heightened. In spring I get a great feeling of renewal and hope seeing the woodland flowers returning to the forest floor regardless of weather, wind, or any other outside factor. In summer they are oases of calm and quiet where the rustling of the leaves promotes a sense of contentment and ease with the world.

But it is probably in autumn that I most feel a sense of spiritual communion. This may be due to the heightened sense of smell at this time, as fungi and wet fallen leaves scent the air. The inevitability of our own decay and death seems not fearful, but part of the natural order of things. Certainly it is at this time that the words of WNP Barbellion, committed to memory at school, come flooding back to me. This extract is from the essay 'An Autumn Stroll' in his book Enjoying Life.

> For, Autumn notwithstanding, the herbage had just reached that stage when it crowds all its many-tinted greens and the whole of its remaining vitality into one last sunny day; then quickly follows death and decay. Even now, a few leaves on that sturdy oak, solitary in the field yonder, have turned to golden russet; the larches, too, overhead are growing ragged and thin, and as the leaves begin to fall a few hardy cones that have weathered one winter already peep from their summer bowers and prepare once more for the blasts.

> In the solemnity and silence of the fir-wood I find an analogy with the atmosphere of mysterious repose in

some stately cathedral, in the midst of, yet apart from the vortex of human life without. Into the dim recesses of the fir-wood few sounds of natural life make their way – except perhaps the call of a crow passing over the tree-tops, or the scream of a startled jay; and these are but momentary. Presently I leave the still woods to pass through the gap in the hedge and so enter the busy whirl of life in the fields.

With best wishes
Éanna Ní Lamhna

ANNE TORMEY

Dear Marie

As far back as I can remember, I would say there was a desire and a longing to know God. I grew up being told about a God who loved me and cared for me, but it made as much sense to be told that pigs could fly, so foreign was the concept to me.

When I would attend Mass on Sundays I would watch the priest, and think, 'Why can I not know God the way this man seems to know him?' Had God got favourites and only let some people come close to him?

When I attempted to ask questions I was told not to question my faith. I would look at Jesus hanging on the cross, and wonder, 'Why in the world did he die such a cruel death?'

I was told, 'This man Jesus died for your sins.' If he did, why did I always feel guilty and have no assurance of my sins having been forgiven no matter how many times I went to confession?

I knew there was an obvious void in my life, and no amount of good deeds, good times, or good things were able to fill that void.

My mother and father did their best with their limited knowledge, to present a God to us whom they desired we would love and follow, but in my teenage years all thoughts of God were lost in the endless dances and parties that I attended.

People would have described me as the life and soul of any party. I had the ability to make people laugh. I was laughing on the outside, but inside I was slowly dying.

I got married at 19 to a wonderful man and for the next few years was kept busy with having a family; also I was trying to come to terms with situations that were occurring in the lives of my brothers in particular.

I am the eldest of 13 children and felt somehow responsible for my brothers and sisters and worried when things started to go wrong in their lives.

In the late seventies heroin hit the streets of Dublin with a vengeance, all over the city boys and girls where getting caught in its grip. Three of my brothers got addicted, one of my brothers later died of AIDS; the other two are living with HIV.

The area where we once lived in Rialto, where we laughed and played, has lost a whole generation to drugs. Some families have lost up to four members. In some ways we count ourselves lucky by comparison.

I would have called myself the fixer in my family. Maybe it has something to do with being the first child, but this was something I could not fix.

This crisis triggered in me a spiritual crisis that caused me to begin to look heavenwards. Every night I would cry out to a God I did not know, for an answer that did eventually come.

My sister Marie, the fourth child in our family, began to tell us about the dramatic change that had taken place in her life. The year was 1987, and she began to tell us that we could know Jesus personally, that we could have a personal relationship with him, and that her life was now transformed because of this relationship with Jesus.

I did not understand all she was telling me, but I only had to look at her to know that a great change had indeed taken place. Something not of this world had had a great effect on her, she had a peace that I craved for, and she talked about God as intimately as one would talk about a lover.

But this lover was the lover of her soul, and his name was Jesus Christ. There's a scripture in the Bible, Jeremiah 29: 13, which says 'You will seek me and find me when you seek me with all of your heart', and that's what I began to do.

The amazing thing was that no-one looking at me from the outside would have realised the turmoil that was in my heart. I still went to work, did the shopping, did my housework, went for a few jars, looked after my four young children. But inside I was longing for answers to my questions.

What was the meaning of this life? Is this all there is? Life seemed so meaningless, so empty, the void in my heart seemed to grow bigger with every passing day. Looking back I now know that God was guiding and directing me, even if my life was out of control, God was in control and was in the driving seat of my life – all I needed to do was follow directions.

My sister Marie invited me to go to the church with her on Sunday. This church is two minutes away from where I live. What had I got to lose? If nothing else it was an opportunity to meet some of my family members who at this time were attending also.

I shall never forget the joy that was present among the people, and the wonderful way they worshipped God. It was evident that they knew God because no one could sing and praise the way they did, unless they were acquainted with the one they were worshipping.

It was here that I learned John 3: 16. 'For God so loved the world he gave his only begotten son, so that whoever believes in him shall not perish but have eternal life.' It was here that I came into a living relationship with Jesus Christ as my Lord and Saviour, because on May 16th 1988 I said a simple prayer asking Jesus who died for me to forgive me of my sins. I asked him to come into my life and give me a fresh start.

I never felt a lightning bolt from heaven, or a booming voice speaking to me. But what I did feel was a great sense of peace. I felt like someone had washed me clean inside. But the best part was I knew the void had been filled. Many times I had read on poster boards, 'You must be born again.' I had never understood what this meant, now I had experienced what it meant.

It was like someone had switched on a light in my spirit, a spirit that was dead until Jesus came in. Now God was so real to me I knew without a shadow of a doubt that he existed and that he loved me. I began to read the Bible, a book I had never understood. It became illuminated to me, it began to make sense. God began to speak to me through what the Bible said.

Prayer became a priority in my life. I could barely get out of bed in the mornings, now I was up at 6.30 before everyone else so I could pray. I started going to Bible studies. So great was my hunger to know God that I think I was going to four a week.

Also, God put a deep desire in my heart to tell others about this Jesus who loves them and died on their behalf, and this desire has not diminished to this day. God has called me to preach and teach and it's a great privilege when I get the opportunity. Twelve members of my immediate family have all professed faith in Jesus, and all of them are still following him today. Each of them could tell their own individual stories of how God has kept them through thick and thin.

Today, eleven years after my encounter with God the fire and passion for him has not grown any dimmer. I love him with all my heart and I know that I will serve him until the day I die.

I have had my ups and downs, my troubles and strifes, but I know he is always with me, he has promised he will never leave me or forsake me no matter what life may bring. His peace is always available to me and to you, dear reader – all you have to do is reach out to him; he is nearer than you can imagine.

Yours sincerely

Anne Tormey

LIZ McMANUS

Dear Marie

Enclosed is the poem as requested. My daughter discovered it and read it at my father's funeral. We live on in our children and in their children. It is a wonderful thing – even a little frightening when you think about it.

Yours sincerely

Liz Mc Manus TD

Heredity

I am the family face;
Flesh perishes, I live on,
Projecting trait and trace
Through time to times anon,
And leaping from place to place
Over oblivion.
The years-heired feature that can
In curve and voice and eye
Despise the human span
Of durance – that is I;
The eternal thing in man,
That heeds no call to die.

THOMAS HARDY (1840–1928)

MURIEL McCARTHY

Dear Marie

I enclose my choice of poems which may be suitable for your publication.

I find John Donne's poems deeply moving. They are also graceful, joyous and harmonious. Donne showed how love unites and its eternal significance. 'The Anniversarie' expresses the most profound emotions of love in all its physical and spiritual aspects.

The medieval prayer 'In my understanding' (from This prymer of Salysbury use, 1538, *author unknown) has been said for hundreds of years and is still said today in many churches in Ireland. It can be used in times of sorrow and joy and it supplies a deep spiritual need. It has been set to music and because it is so simple it can be used by children and adults.*

Even more helpful and simple is the prayer 'O angel of God' which is widely known and loved and is taught to almost every child in Ireland.

Kind regards

Yours sincerely
Muriel McCarthy

The Anniversarie

All Kings, and all their favourites,
All glory of honors, beauties, wits,
The Sun it selfe, which makes times, as they passe,
Is elder by a yeare, now, then it was
When thou and I first one another saw:
All other things, to their destruction draw,
Only our love hath no decay;
This, no to morrow hath, nor yesterday,
Running it never runs from us away,
But truly keepes his first, last, everlasting day.

Two graves must hide thine and my coarse,
      If one might, death were no divorce.
Alas, as well as other Princes, wee,
(Who Prince enough in one another bee,)
Must leave at last in death, these eyes, and eares,
Oft fed with true oathes, and with sweet salt teares;
      But soules where nothing dwells but love
(All other thoughts being inmates) then shall prove
This, or a love increased there above,
When bodies to their graves, soules from their graves remove.

      And then we shall be thoroughly blest,
      But wee no more, then all the rest;
Here upon earth, we'are Kings, and none but wee
Can be such Kings, nor of such subjects bee.
Who is so safe as wee? where none can doe
Treason to us, except one of us two.
      True and false feares let us refraine,
Let us love nobly, and live, and adde againe
Yeares and yeares unto yeares, till we attaine
To write threescore: this is the second of our raigne.

JOHN DONNE (1573–1631)

O, angel of God, my guardian dear
To whom God's love commits me here,
Ever this day be at my side
To light, to guard, to rule and guide.
Amen

This Prymer of Salysbury use...

God be in my hede
      And in myn understandynge
God be in my eyen
      And in my lokynge
God be in my mouth
      And in myn spekynge
God be in my herte
      And in my thynkynge
God be at myn ende
      And at my departynge.

TOM STACK

Dear Marie

In response to someone's callow inquiry 'What is jazz?' Louis Armstrong is said to have famously replied 'If you've gotta ask, you'll never know!' Somewhat the same principle may apply to the understanding of poetry. Its mode is not discursive. It strikes notes that stir the imagination and sounds chords that travel beyond the confines of rational discourse. Unlike prose it comes with a special charge that reaches right to the marrow. Several of Patrick Kavanagh's poems have been, for me, both enlightening and affecting. Curiously, it is sometimes difficult to explain exactly why. Perhaps his attraction for me lies in his poetic matrix of farm and field which I associate with charmed holidays of my own youth in County Clare, from which I can recall with pleasure the scenes, events and even mini-epiphanies – 'The view that happened to no one else but me' – that are the stuff of Kavanagh's contemplative excursions; churns, harrows, straw-stuffed saddles, cut-away bogs, turkeys' secret eggs – 'the undying difference in the corner of a field,' unkempt water and the immortality of grass.' Ruminations on such as these were also part of my rural repertoire. Another reason why Kavanagh is important to me is that he gets to the quick of my Christianity: 'You have not got a chance with fraud/and might as well be true to God,' 'and (I) have learned with surprise that God unworshipped withers to the Futile One,' 'we must not dream tomorrow's judgement/God must be allowed to surprise us.' These sharp counsels although elementary remain always in season.

Patrick Kavanagh insisted that poetry 'had to do with the reality of the Spirit, of faith and hope and sometimes charity'. His poetry puts images to work in an enterprise of discovery. His allusive lines are replete with details of rural activities and events from which he manages to move ingeniously to expressions of universal experience. Seamus Heaney remarks 'it is when his ethereal literary voice incarnates itself in the imagery of the actual world that its message of transcendence becomes credible.' Putting this, as Kavanagh so often does, in a Catholic Christian context endows all created reality with something of the holiness of God. This matching of the material

*with the spiritual is called sacramentality. A sacramental perspective
is one that 'sees' the divine in the human, the infinite in the finite,
the eternal in the historical. This must never be mistaken for some
kind of idolatry, pantheism or magic. True sacramentalism confers
an instinct by which we recognise all reality as sacred – 'God in the
bits and pieces of everyday.' Sacramentalism does not tamper with
the integrity of creation, nor does it sentimentalise its subject. It
simply reads reality in a special way, enhancing it by eliciting signs
of richness and satisfaction from the material universe and the play
of human events.*

*The poem 'Advent' is a meditation on the Nativity in which
Kavanagh builds up the sense of mystery and wonder, as the
Christian prepares for the coming of the Saviour. Once that event
takes place, God's presence amongst his people will be renewed. The
recharging of Creation with the Divine Presence puts 'newness in
every stale thing'. This transformation is not heralded by any
spectacular cosmic interruption but naturally, modestly, even
imperceptibly, while life goes on as usual 'pouring ordinary plenty' –
old men chat on, young lads hang about and the routine of dairying
continues. A new experience steals into our world with the Nativity
event and all becomes invested with the freshness that belongs to a
child's innocent vision and signals the recovery of wonder. A new
order is being wrought for us by virtue of the mystery of the
Incarnation – earth and flesh touched and endeared by God's own
life. Fertility and the life of the earth are poetically harnessed to
suggest the regeneration of the human spirit.*

*Above all, the poem 'Advent' offers a play between nostalgia and
longing ('charm back the luxury/Of a child's soul', 'Won't we be
rich, my love and I, and please/God we shall not ask for reason's
payment'). There is the evocation of a cherished past along with the
expectation of an enriched future. This may be read as an exploration
of memory and hope, major constituents of all our lives. My present
life sits between memory and hope; what has gone before and what
has yet to come. I am shaped by my past experience, my personal
story. All of this is fed by memory; the people I have known, the
events I have witnessed, what I have done and what I have failed to
do. I await my future and this anticipation is grounded in hope; a
hope that I would like to think chimes with Kavanagh's own sense of
hope which for him emerges from paradox. Prone to failure as we are,
it is, nevertheless, as he says 'failure of a kind'. The human being is*

ultimately indestructible, precisely because of his or her
vulnerability – 'undefeatable by means of the beatable,' as he
pronounces in another poem of his, 'The Self-Slaved', I would settle
for this credo.

Very Rev Tom Stack

Advent

We have tested and tasted too much, lover –
Through a chink too wide there comes in no wonder,
But here in the Advent-darkened room
Where the dry bread and the sugarless tea
Of penance will charm back the luxury
Of a child's soul, we'll return to Doom
The knowledge we stole but could not use.

And the newness that was in every stale thing
When we looked at it as children; the spirit-shocking
Wonder in a black slanting Ulster hill
Or the prophetic astonishment in the tedious talking
Of an old fool will awake for us and bring
You and me to the yard gate to watch the whins
And the bog-holes, cart-tracks, old stables where Time begins.

O after Christmas we'll have no need to go searching
For the difference that sets an old phrase burning –
We'll hear it in the whispered argument of a churning
Or in the streets where the village boys are lurching.
And we'll hear it among decent men too
Who barrow dung in gardens under trees,
Wherever life pours ordinary plenty.

Won't we be rich, my love and I, and please
God we shall not ask for reason's payment,
The why of heart-breaking strangeness in dreeping hedges
Nor analyse God's breath in common statement.
We have thrown into the dust-bin the clay-minted wages
Of pleasure, knowledge and the conscious hour –
And Christ comes with a January flower.

Patrick Kavanagh (1904–67)

EVELYN CONLON

Dear Marie

I've been looking at these words 'spiritual sustenance' and they puzzle me because I don't know what 'spiritual' means. Of course I know the dictionary definition but I'm out of touch with a public meaning. I do know that spirituality couldn't be about some of the guff that I was force fed when growing up. It must be about morality, which is all about politics in the sense that 'politics' can be a pure word just as 'spirituality' can be. And the spirit must also have a laugh, so instead of burdening you with what I murmur to myself when I'm cornered in a field by a kicking horse, how's this for lip exercise?

Evelyn Conlon

There is a certain glandular disturbance all beautiful, wizardy, great people have second sight to, that trumpets through the clothes, sets the nerves up for the kill, and torments the senses to orange explosure. It has something to do with the cosmic interrelationship between the cellular attunement of certain designated organs and the firmental correlation with the axis shifts of the globe. My mother calls it sex and my brother says it's groin-fever time. But then they were always ones for brevity.

Toni Cade Bambera (1939–)

PROINNSÍAS Ó DUINN

Greetings and best wishes to all in Town House
'If music be the food of love, play on.'

In his vast output, Shakespeare provides us with many very astute observations on life and the psychology of human behaviour, but this particular quote moves in on the area that would put the great man himself out of business. It raises the whole question of being able to reach into the depths of human emotions and relationships without uttering a word. Even better, without thinking in language. As a conductor I fully appreciate the advantages in communicating directly with the soul and heart without having to resort to words that can be so easily distorted or misinterpreted.

While being aware of many of the pearls of wisdom to be found in theatre and on the book shelf, I have been most profoundly affected by two sentences which were said in my presence by relatively faceless people and one which I read on a poster in a small country restaurant. I suppose, like many things in life, it is all a matter of timing.

'You are not responsible for a person's actions. You are only responsible for your own reactions.' This came at a time early in my career when I was finding the stance and rudeness of some of the people I encountered to be quite unacceptable. I found it equally upsetting to be in the presence of anyone treating a third party with anything but dignity and respect. Applying my new-found maxim to specifics immediately turned my whole attitude around. By controlling my own reactions I found myself in a position where I was not only less offended on such occasions but in a better position to counter from a more objective and calmer perspective.

'There are no bad people – at least as long as you don't think about them.' There was a slight pause between these two phrases, enough for me to conjure up a hit list of names ranging from colleagues through national and international politicians I felt the world could do without. Then I focused on the second part. I have always found it disturbing to see the number of people who spend their time in the canteen at work or on the phone to their friends complaining about their bosses, their work colleagues, or acquaintances. All this

negativity is on their own valuable time which they will never get back. One cannot deny that less than desirable people are out there and many of them do indeed manage to get into positions of authority. The trick is to keep them out of your personal space. I suppose I had frequently heard the expression 'out of sight, out of mind' but this particular way of expressing it made me focus more sharply. In a way it reminded me of the over simplification of Toscanini's answer to the question 'What is the art of conducting?' – 'Finding the tune!'

During my lunch I noticed a picture on the far wall of the restaurant. It was a tranquil painting of a coastline complete with the traditional sea gulls (if they ever joined Equity they would make a fortune!) sweeping bay, and setting sun on the water. When I went to leave I passed close enough to read the sentence at the bottom – 'You will never reach new horizons unless you have the courage to leave the shore.' In my own profession this can be taken literally. Its dynamic is far more dramatic, however, when applied to the mind. The process of not just accepting information and interpretations passed on to me by adults during my formative years opened up leading the way to a whole fresh freedom of thought and the strength to question, discard, form and act upon my own views and beliefs. Not always easy, but essential.

I shouldn't be surprised that I was influenced by these encounters because they are very much in line with my belief in the power of positive thinking. The creative artist who makes his audience smile is the one I admire most.

Proinnsías Ó Duinn

TIM ROBINSON

Dear Marie Heaney

Thanks for inviting me to contribute to your book in aid of Focus Ireland. I enclose an object of contemplation and a brief explanation of it, which I hope you will find suitable.

Most positive whole numbers can be written as the product of smaller numbers; for instance, 15=3 x 5. Prime numbers are those that cannot be broken down like this; they are the indivisible atoms of arithmetic. The list gives the first 210 primes. This sequence thins out; there are 25 primes among the first hundred whole numbers, but only six between 100,000 and 100,100. Among really huge numbers one could search through millions without finding a prime, and then one will turn up, like the biggest prime discovered to date (as of November 1998) which has over 900,000 digits and would fill a 300-page book. Teams of mathematicians are racing to calculate even bigger ones, but their task will never come to an end, for the sequence of primes goes on forever (a fact that was known to Euclid in 300 BC), like a line of monoliths, each taller than the last, leading beyond all horizons. And there is no formula for it, no pattern. For instance, although in general the gaps between primes get bigger, every now and then a pair occurs close together, like 104471 and 104473. It has been conjectured that there is an infinite number of such pairs of primes differing only by two; however, this is one of many seemingly simple statements about primes which have never been proved.

The most profound mathematical theorem of the twentieth century (if not of the second millennium) is Gödel's proof that not even arithmetic can be reduced to a system, that whatever basis one starts from, there will be true arithmetical statements that cannot be proved from that basis. Perhaps the way this unknowability enters into mathematics (and into all logical thought of any complexity) is through the primes. If so, the sequence of primes is an endless seam of stitches joining reason to the incomprehensible. In fact, if the physicists are right in thinking that the ultimate constituents of matter and energy are numerical in nature, then the mystery of the primes is the prime mystery.

Yours sincerely

Tim Robinson

The Sequence of Primes

2 3 5 7 11 13 17 19 23 29 31 37 41 43 47 53 59 61 67 71
73 79 83 89 97 101 103 107 109 113 127 131 137 139 149
151 157 163 167 173 179 181 191 193 197 199 211 223 227
229 233 239 241 251 257 263 269 271 277 281 283 293 307
311 313 317 331 337 347 349 353 359 367 373 379 383 389
397 401 409 419 421 431 433 439 443 449 457 461 463 467
479 487 491 499 503 509 521 523 541 547 557 563 569 571
577 587 593 599 601 607 613 617 619 631 641 643 647 653
659 661 673 677 683 691 701 709 719 727 733 739 743 751
757 761 769 773 787 797 809 811 821 823 827 829 839 853
857 859 863 877 881 883 887 907 911 919 929 937 941 947
953 967 971 977 983 991 997 1009 1013 1019 1021 1031
1033 1039 1049 1051 1061 1063 1069 1087 1091 1093 1097
1103 1109 1117 1123 1129 1151 1153 1163 1171 1181 1187
1193 1201 1213 1217 1223 1229 1231 1237 1249 1259 1277
1279 1283 1289 1291...

MARY HENRY

Dear Marie

As a child most of the classical music I had heard was of the Bach, Beethoven and Brahms variety. Trips from school to hear the Hallé Orchestra in Cork City Hall were highlights of my musical education.

Arriving in Trinity, even though I longed to be there, was quite a terrifying experience – new city, ancient buildings, no old friends but a wonderful new one called Rosemary. She, from Donegal, was as lonely and nervous as I was but that first week we took courage in our hands and set off for the Gramophone Society on the top floor of No. 6 in Front Square.

Dvořák's New World Symphony was the first offering of the session. I had never knowingly heard it before and felt it expressed all that could be said about leaving the familiar and entering the unknown. The strong triumphant opening with plenty of percussion made the statement of arrival so confident. A longing for times past was repeated by woodwinds and strings so that the constant repetition was reassuring and familiar after a while. Trumpets made the refrain firm and there was fresh urgency in the strings bringing us forward.

Those following movements of thoughtful largo with the soulful oboe holding the refrain, on to the jolly singing scherzo, triangles and strings dancing on into the final movement which positively races to a final firm decisive confluence of all the sections of the orchestra backed by the kettle drums are my best support in times of crisis or distress. It's one of the most positive pieces of music I know.

Sadly, Rosemary died a long time ago but that night as we went back up Grafton Street and the Green to our digs in Harcourt Street our shoulders were back, there were smiles on our faces, the future looked good. A Czech had given confidence to a girl from Cork and her chum from Donegal.

With love

Mary

DESMOND EGAN

Dear Marie

Thank you for asking me to be involved in such a worthy project. I am happy that royalties go to Focus Ireland.

I have a wide interest in the arts and, since you ask, I find sustenance for my (battered) spirit from many of them. .

Music does matter: how greedily I listen every day and how much it helps! The playing of Swedish pianist Hans Palsson – for me, the greatest living pianist – has really meant a lot to me over the past five or six years. So have the songs of poor Schubert; of Hugo Wolf, and of Richard Strauss (especially his four last). For me, too, the music and performance of Thelonius Monk, that weird jazz musician, has calories and spiritual vitamins in it. Ditto, the fiddling of Tommy Peoples – a genuine traditional player in an era of riverdancing, bouzouki- and guitar-clowning.

In painting, I am cheered and lifted by the likes of Mark Rothko and Giorgio Morandi – whose reverence for things could leave the latter agitated even in the face of a bottle. The sculpture of Giacometti and of our own wonderful artist, James McKenna, mean a lot to me: the work of such rare souls makes us all more alive. And so, speaking for myself, do some of those wonderful Greek sculptures (two of which I have in my study) from the 6th and 5th centuries BC respectively – though I like equally well the later, Hellenistic style, and its battle with a sense of chaos which we can recognise in our own time. Ikons are arguably the most spiritual of all art and it is no accident that my favourite filmmaker, the Russian Alexander Tarkovsky, created his masterpiece on the theme of that great ikon-maker of the 15th century, Andrei Rubljev. I watch this film from time to time and never fail to get a lift from it.

But maybe what you need for this anthology is not a general statement but a particular text? Not easy. In that case, I would have to bypass some favourites. Patrick Kavanagh, for one, whose, 'Dandelions growing on headlands, showing/Their unloved hearts to everyone' are a lot more than dandelions.

I would also have to leave out George Herbert and 'Love'; Simone Weil, a permanent inspiration, who wrote, for example, that,

'I believe in the responsibility of the writers of recent years for the disaster of our time.' Wow! Who thinks like that nowadays? Thoreau, as well, would have to go, whose words, 'Our life is frittered away by detail... Simplify, simplify... To a philosopher all news as it is called, is gossip, and they who edit and read it are old women over their tea.' And others such (in Walden*) both inspire and console.*

I would even pass Gerard Manley Hopkins, who wrote, '...for Christ plays in ten thousand places,/Lovely in limbs, and lovely in eyes not his...'

– Yes: I would, if I must, forego the company of such old friends (who telephone me regularly) in favour of the words and acts of that same Christ, beautiful, profound, and touching as he was and remains. The four Gospels nourish my spirit more than anything or anybody else. In a much later poem which Hopkins wrote in Monasterevin, Co Kildare, he simply says, 'There's none but truth can stead you. Christ is truth.'

This is my sustenance as I grow older and try, like Thoreau, to face up to life and discover what it all amounts to, if anything. No one makes the kind of sense that Christ makes; sees more deeply, or has more compassion for us wanderers:

> 'Not on bread alone does man live.'
> 'The truth will set you free.'
> 'Forgive us our offences as we in turn forgive those who offend us.'

No one matters more to me.

Warm regards

As ever

Desmond Egan

MARTIN DRURY

Dear Marie

Thank you for asking me to contribute to your book. The brief you set is a difficult one but I am hanging onto one key word which you employ twice in your letter of invitation: sustenance.

Having been, until my early twenties, a devout and obedient Roman Catholic, I can still recall the seismic shock (and indeed can still experience the aftershocks) of the opening up of the fault-line between orthodox religious practice and authentic spiritual experience.

I deplore greatly that those who were so quick to claim me for their own church were so slow to nourish my individual spiritual self. Abandoning the orthodoxies meant and still means going on a personal journey. Those who charged themselves with my spiritual formation, and who were in truth more concerned with finding than with seeking, gave me no map-making skills by which I could chart my journey. The cartography I have grown to admire and trust and which I find sustaining is that employed by artists of all disciplines.

If music is the food of love, then faith and hope are nourished also by music and the other arts. If the greatest of these is perhaps love, then maybe that is in part because music is perhaps the greatest of the arts. Certainly my belief in heaven will be greatly sustained if, as I pass away, I hear Monteverdi's Chiome D'Oro *sung by Emma Kirkby and Evelyn Tubb.*

But spiritual sustenance is by no means only of the uplifting variety. For we are terrestrial creatures, made of flesh and blood, and our spiritual selves are surely mapped onto that flesh with the marks made by artists, composers and writers. If I were ever asked to summarise the bible, I'd say that it was a story in two parts. The first is a post-modern novel about the failure of words. Opening with 'In the beginning was the Word,' it proceeds to describe words on tablets of stone; words being written on a wall by a moving finger; words being spoken through a burning bush. The failure of these words is announced at the end of the first part of the narrative in a kind of trailer to the second part which will be presented as a film script: an action-based thriller in which 'the Word was made flesh and dwelt amongst us'.

Whether announced from on high or made flesh on earth, certainly words are central. My preference is for the ambiguous cartography of literature and for the celebration of humanity rather than some remote divinity. Because I do not share the cynicism of our age nor am I (any more) a card-carrying optimist, I am drawn to texts which explore the richness of the human condition and all our many interconnected selves, the spiritual among them. That is why the text to which I return again and again for spiritual sustenance is a testament by the great American poet Walt Whitman: Song of Myself. *It is a poem long and wide, like some great American river, and you can dip in it, bathe in it, drink from it, or, as I wish to do now, carry some of it to others for their sustenance. Three cupfuls is all I crave on behalf of your readers, in the hope that they will be moved to seek out its fullness for themselves.*

With best wishes for the success of this publication. I look forward to feeding off the sustenance provided by all your contributors.

Sincerely
Martin Drury

from Song of Myself

1

I celebrate myself, and sing myself,
And what I assume you shall assume,
For every atom belonging to me as good belongs to you.
I loafe and invite my soul,
I lean and loafe at my ease observing a spear of summer
grass.

My tongue, every atom of my blood, form'd from this soil,
this air,
Born here of parents born here from parents the same, and
their parents the same,
I, now thirty-seven years old in perfect health begin,
Hoping to cease not till death.

Creeds and schools in abeyance,
Retiring back a while sufficed at what they are, but never
forgotten,
I harbour for good or bad, I permit to speak at every hazard,
Nature without check with original energy.

3

I have heard what the talkers were talking, the talk of the
beginning and the end,
But I do not talk of the beginning or the end.

There was never any more inception than there is now,
Nor any more youth or age than there is now,
And will never be any more perfection than there is now,
Nor any more heaven or hell than there is now.

Urge and urge and urge,
Always the procreant urge of the world.

Out of the dimness opposite equals advance, always
substance and increase,
Always sex,
Always a knit of identity, always distinction, always a breed
of life.
To elaborate is no avail, learn'd and unlearn'd feel that it is so.

Sure as the most certain sure, plumb in the uprights, well
entretied, braced in the beams,
Stout as a horse, affectionate, haughty, electrical,
I and this mystery here we stand.

Clear and sweet is my soul, and clear and sweet is all that is
not my soul.

Lack one lacks both, and the unseen is proved by the seen,
Till that becomes unseen and receives proof in its turn.

17

These are really the thoughts of all men in all ages and lands,
they are
Not original with me,
If they are not yours as much as mine they are nothing, or
next to nothing,

If they are not the riddle and the untying of the riddle they
are nothing,
If they are not just as close as they are distant they are
nothing.

This is the grass that grows wherever the land is and the
water is,
This is the common air that bathes the globe.

WALT WHITMAN (1819–92)

SUSAN McKENNA-LAWLOR

Dear Ms Heaney

Thank you very much for the compliment of inviting me to provide an input to the book you are preparing on 'paths to spiritual sustenance'.

Spiritual sustenance can for me be attained through my work as a scientist and this process is, to some extent, reflected in the attached words:

> Inaudible to our deaf mortal ears
> The wide world-rhythms
> Wove their stupendous chant
> To which life strives to fit our rhyme-beats here,
> Melting our limits in the illimitable,
> Tuning the finite to infinity.
>
> SRI AUROBINDO GHOSE

With every kind wish.

Sincerely yours

(Prof) Susan McKenna-Lawlor

PAUL BRADY

Dear Marie

I would be delighted to contribute to your collection. What I would like to offer is a poem by George Russell (AE) which had a profound effect on me at a time (early 80s) when I was trying to make sense of what it felt like to be Irish against the back-drop of the hunger strikes. I had been struggling with the writing of my song 'The Island' and to stumble across Russell's poem 'On Behalf of Some Irishmen Not Followers of Tradition' in the periodical The Crane Bag *was like a light in the dark. My particular context was that I had spent much of the previous decade involved in traditional music and song and was beginning to realise that while I loved this part of being Irish – this part of me – I didn't share a lot of the other easy assumptions that frequently came with the territory. The emotional confusion that followed was considerably eased by the discovery that decades before me someone had articulated a lot of what I was now feeling. I remained and still remain strongly attached to the cultural 'splendour of the Gael' and that part of me that shares in it. But the thought that it was OK to try and maybe add to it, become something else, re-invent oneself, even, and still be Irish was and still is an exciting and liberating concept.*

I hope this is not too 'political' a concept for your book. It's hard sometimes to know where the dividing lines between politics and matters of the spirit are.

Yours sincerely

Paul Brady

On Behalf of Some Irishmen Not Followers of Tradition

They call us aliens, we are told,
Because our wayward visions stray
From that dim banner they unfold
The dreams of worn-out yesterday.
The sum of all the past is theirs,

The creeds, the deeds, the fame, the name,
Whose death-created glory flares
And dims the spark of living flame.
They weave the necromancer's spell,
And burst the graves where martyrs slept,
Their ancient story to retell,
Renewing tears the dead have wept.
And they would have us join their dirge,
This worship of an extinct fire
In which they drift beyond the verge
Where races all outworn expire.
The worship of the dead is not
A worship that our hearts allow,
Though every famous shade were wrought
With woven thorns above the brow.
We fling our answer back in scorn:
'We are less children of the clime
Than of some nation yet unborn
Or empire in the womb of time.
We hold the Ireland in the heart
More than the land our eyes have seen,
And love the goal for which we start
More than the tale of what has been.'
The generations as they rise
May live the life men lived before,
Still hold the thought once held as wise,
Go in and out by the same door.
We leave the easy peace it brings:
The few we are shall still unite
In fealty to unseen kings
Or unimaginable light.
We would no Irish sign efface,
But yet our lips would gladlier hail
The Firstborn of the Coming Race
Than the last splendour of the Gael.
No blazoned banner we unfold –
One charge alone we give to youth,
Against the sceptred myth to hold
The golden heresy of truth.

GEORGE RUSSELL (AE) (1867–1935)

PATRICK MASON

Dear Marie

Thank you for your invitation to participate in your new book.

I have found it extremely difficult to come up with anything that I am actually prepared to share because, as you rightly point out, this is a very personal and private area.

However, I would offer the statue scene from Shakespeare's **The Winter's Tale**. *It may not be the kind of text that makes any sense in such a collection, but what it represents on stage is something that I find intensely moving and sustaining. What more can I say, except that 'If this be magic, let it be an art / Lawful as eating.'*

Kind regards.

Yours sincerely
Patrick Mason

The Winter's Tale

Act 5 Scene 3

LEONTES   O grave and good Paulina, the great comfort
That I have had of thee!

PAULINA   What, sovereign sir,
I did not well, I meant well. All my services
You have paid home, but that you have vouchsafed
With your crowned brother and these young contracted
Heirs of your kingdoms my poor house to visit,
It is a surplus of your grace which never
My life may last to answer.

LEONTES   O Paulina,
We honour you with trouble. But we came
To see the statue of our queen. Your gallery
Have we passed through, not without much content

In many singularities; but we saw not
That which my daughter came to look upon,
The statue of her mother.

PAULINA   As she lived peerless,
So her dead likeness I do well believe
Excels what ever yet you looked upon,
Or hand of man hath done. Therefore I keep it
Lonely, apart. But here it is. Prepare
To see the life as lively mocked as ever
Still sleep mocked death. Behold, and say 'tis well.

> *She draws a curtain and reveals the figure of Hermione,*
> *standing like a statue*

I like your silence; it the more shows off
Your wonder. But yet speak; first you, my liege.
Comes it not something near?

LEONTES   Her natural posture.
Chide me, dear stone, that I may say indeed
Thou art Hermione; or rather, thou art she
In thy not chiding, for she was as tender
As infancy and grace. But yet, Paulina,
Hermione was not so much wrinkled, nothing
So aged as this seems.

POLIXENES   O, not by much.

PAULINA   So much the more our carver's excellence,
Which lets go by some sixteen years, and makes her
As she lived now.

LEONTES   As now she might have done,
So much to my good comfort as it is
Now piercing to my soul. O, thus she stood,
Even with such life of majesty – warm life,
As now it coldly stands – when first I wooed her.
I am ashamed. Does not the stone rebuke me
For being more stone than it? O royal piece!
There's magic in thy majesty, which has
My evils conjured to remembrance, and
From thy admiring daughter took the spirits,
Standing like stone with thee.

PERDITA   And give me leave,
And do not say 'tis superstition, that
I kneel and then implore her blessing. Lady,
Dear Queen, that ended when I but began,
Give me that hand of yours to kiss.

PAULINA   O, patience!
The statue is but newly fixed; the colour's
Not dry.

CAMILLO (to Leontes)
My lord, your sorrow was too sore laid on,
Which sixteen winters cannot blow away,
So many summers dry. Scarce any joy
Did ever so long live; no sorrow
But killed itself much sooner.

POLIXENES (to Leontes)   Dear my brother,
Let him that was the cause of this have power
To take off so much grief from you as he
Will piece up in himself.

PAULINA (to Leontes)   Indeed, my lord,
If I had thought the sight of my poor image
Would thus have wrought you – for the stone is mine –
I'd not have showed it.

       She makes to draw the curtain

LEONTES   Do not draw the curtain.

PAULINA   No longer shall you gaze on't, lest your fancy
May think anon it moves.

LEONTES   Let be, let be!
Would I were dead but that methinks already.
What was he that did make it? See, my lord,
Would you not deem it breathed, and that those veins
Did verily bear blood?

POLIXENES   Masterly done.
The very life seems warm upon her lip.

LEONTES
The fixture of her eye has motion in't,
As we are mocked with art.

PAULINA   I'll draw the curtain.
My lord's almost so far transported that
He'll think anon it lives.

LEONTES   O sweet Paulina,
Make me to think so twenty years together.
No settled senses of the world can match
The pleasure of that madness. Let't alone.

PAULINA   I am sorry, sir, I have thus far stirred you; but
I could afflict you farther.

LEONTES   Do, Paulina,
For this affliction has a taste as sweet
As any cordial comfort. Still methinks
There is an air comes from her. What fine chisel
Could ever yet cut breath? Let no man mock me,
For I will kiss her.

PAULINA   Good my lord, forbear.
The ruddiness upon her lip is wet.
You'll mar it if you kiss it, stain your own
With oily painting. Shall I draw the curtain?

LEONTES   No, not these twenty years.

PERDITA   So long could I
Stand by, a looker-on.

PAULINA   Either forbear,
Quit presently the chapel, or resolve you
For more amazement. If you can behold it,
I'll make the statue move indeed, descend,
And take you by the hand. But then you'll think –
Which I protest against – I am assisted
By wicked powers.

LEONTES   What you can make her do
I am content to look on; what to speak,
I am content to hear; for 'tis as easy
To make her speak as move.

PAULINA   It is required
You do awake your faith. Then, all stand still.
Or those that think it is unlawful business
I am about, let them depart.

LEONTES   Proceed.
No foot shall stir.

PAULINA   Music; awake her; strike!

    Music

(*To Hermione*)   'Tis time. Descend. Be stone no more.
                      Approach.
Strike all that look upon with marvel. Come,
I'll fill your grave up. Stir. Nay, come away.
Bequeath to death your numbness, for from him
Dear life redeems you.
(*To Leontes*)   You perceive she stirs.

    Hermione slowly descends

Start not. Her actions shall be holy as
You hear my spell is lawful. Do not shun her
Until you see her die again, for then
You kill her double. Nay, present your hand.
When she was young, you wooed her. Now, in age,
Is she become the suitor?

LEONTES   O, she's warm!
If this be magic let it be an art
Lawful as eating.

POLIXENES   She embraces him.

CAMILLLO   She hangs about his neck.
If she pertain to life, let her speak too.

POLIXENES   Ay, and make it manifest where she has lived,
Or how stol'n from the dead.

PAULINA   That she is living,
Were it but told you, should be hooted at
Like an old tale. But it appears she lives,
Though yet she speak not. Mark a little while.
(*To Perdita*)   Please you to interpose, fair madam.
Kneel,
And pray your mother's blessing. – Turn, good lady,
Our Perdita is found.

HERMIONE   You gods, look down,
And from your sacred vials pour your graces

Upon my daughter's head. – Tell me, mine own,
Where hast thou been preserved? Where lived? How found
Thy father's court? For thou shalt hear that I,
Knowing by Paulina that the oracle
Gave hope thou wast in being, have preserved
Myself to see the issue.

PAULINA   There's time enough for that,
Lest they desire upon this push to trouble
Your joys with like relation. Go together,
You precious winners all; your exultation
Partake to everyone. I, an old turtle,
Will wing me to some withered bough, and there
My mate, that's never to be found again,
Lament till I am lost.

LEONTES   O peace, Paulina!
Thou shouldst a husband take by my consent,
As I by thine a wife. This is a match,
And made between's by vows. Thou hast found mine,
But how is to be questioned, for I saw her,
As I thought, dead, and have in vain said many
A prayer upon her grave. I'll not seek far –
For him, I partly know his mind – to find thee
An honourable husband. Come, Camillo,
And take her by the hand, whose worth and honesty
Is richly noted, and here justified
By us, a pair of kings. Let's from this place.
(*To Hermione*) What, look upon my brother. Both your
pardons,
That e'er I put between your holy looks
My ill suspicion. This your son-in-law
And son unto the King, whom heavens directing
Is troth-plight to your daughter. Good Paulina,
Lead us from hence, where we may leisurely
Each one demand and answer to his part
Performed in this wide gap of time since first
We were dissevered. Hastily lead away.

WILLIAM SHAKESPEARE (1564–1616)

'Spiritual sustenance involves that feeling
of a perfect match between what is needed
and what has been supplied. The feeling of
a gap closing and at the same time,
equally and paradoxically, of a space
opening. It seems at those moments that
we are made for illumination. Something
that we needed to be sure of is entering us
and yet it also feels as if it is being
located somewhere deep inside us.'

Seamus Heaney

'Better a dinner of herbs where love is
than a stalled ox and hatred therewith.'

Quoted from the Bible by
Bernadette Madden

'Nature is the oldest scripture.'

John O'Donohue

'What nourishes and sustains my
understanding and my imagination
sustains my spirit.'

Ciarán Benson

'God's love is free equally for all the
people of the world.'

Very Rev David Kerr,
President of the Methodist Church in
Ireland

'People's goodness as it shows itself in
their acts... of justice and solidarity,
compassion and kindness, is infinitely
more important to me than faith in
God...'

Andy Pollak

'It is possible to suffer with dignity and
without.'

Etty Hillesum, quoted by
Michael O'Siadhail

GERALD DAVIS

Dear Marie

Thanks for inviting me to submit a piece for your book of spiritual sustenances.

When I was in Australia some years ago I saw an exhibition of works by Michael Leunig in the Adelaide Art Gallery. I was immediately struck by the marvellous melancholy of his drawings. Ostensibly a cartoonist, his work, whilst deceptively simple, goes far beyond humour and contains its own gentle philosophy of love and spirituality. In his book Short Notes From The Long History of Happiness, *in addition to his drawings, there are several short poems and prose pieces. This is one of my favourites:*

God help us to live slowly:
To move simply:
To look softly:
To allow emptiness:
To let the heart create for us.

Amen

As to my spirituality? I attended a talk by a woman called Catherine Ingram about a year ago. She quoted a Zen master's dictum: 'Be Quiet'. It's as simple as that!

All the best

Gerald

MILO O'SHEA

Dear Marie

As a youth I hated the works of WB Yeats – because I was forced to study him at school. It was only when I started performing Yeats in the theatre in such plays as Words Upon the Window Pane *and* Purgatory *that I began to appreciate his greatness.*

I am not a particularly religious man but life – and the various roles I've played I think – have made me a rather spiritual one. The priests – the rabbis – the saints – the villains – people in life's everyday situations that I have been privileged to create have, I feel, led me back to Yeats and to one of his most touching and beautiful poems – 'The Ballad of Father Gilligan'.

Milo O'Shea

The Ballad of Father Gilligan

The old priest Peter Gilligan
Was weary night and day;
For half his flock were in their beds,
Or under green sods lay.

Once, while he nodded on a chair,
At the moth-hour of eve,
Another poor man sent for him,
And he began to grieve.

'I have no rest, nor joy, nor peace,
For people die and die';
And after cried he, 'God forgive!
My body spake, not I!'

He knelt, and leaning on the the chair
He prayed and fell asleep;
And the moth-hour went from the fields,
And stars began to peep.

They slowly into millions grew,
And leaves shook in the wind;
And God covered the world with shade,
And whispered to mankind.

Upon the time of sparrow-chirp
When the moths came once more,
The old priest Peter Gilligan
Stood upright on the floor.

'Mavrone, mavrone! The man has died
While I slept on the chair';
He roused his horse out of its sleep,
And rode with little care.

He rode now as he never rode,
By rocky lane and fen;
The sick man's wife opened the door:
'Father! You come again!'

'And is the poor man dead?' he cried.
'He died an hour ago.'
The old priest Peter Gilligan
In grief swayed to and fro.

'When you were gone, he turned and died
As merry as a bird.'
The old priest Peter Gilligan
He knelt him at that word.

'He Who hath made the night of stars
For souls who tire and bleed,
Sent one of His great angels down
To help me in my need.

He Who is wrapped in purple robes,
With planets in His care,
Had pity on the least of things
Asleep upon a chair.'

WB YEATS (1865–1939)

JOHN QUINN

Ah now Marie! there's a question! 'What is it that gives you spiritual sustenance...?' I could try to be clever and give you a one-word answer – LIFE! – but I'll try to tease it out a bit further.

Patrick Kavanagh said it much better:

> God is in the bits and pieces of Everyday -
> A kiss here and a laugh again, and sometimes tears
> A pearl necklace round the neck of poverty.

(PATRICK KAVANAGH, FROM 'THE GREAT HUNGER')

This attempt at an answer will never wander too far from Kavanagh. In his earthliest moments he is, for me, the most spiritual of writers.

Part of my affinity for Kavanagh is rooted in the fact that my father came from the wee hills of Monaghan. Although he became a garda sergeant he never really left the land. In the days when the greatest crimes in a County Meath village were unlighted bikes and noxious weeds, there was ample time for a garda sergeant to be a part-time farmer. So we kept a couple of cows, a pig or two, some calves, hens, turkeys, grew our own potatoes and turnips, saved our own hay and turf. What does all that have to do with spiritual sustenance? Again, Kavanagh replies: 'Clay is the word and clay is the flesh...'

To be intimate with soil and growth and regeneration is the most fundamental form of spiritual nourishment. And to be with animals is equally sustaining. To stand in a stall, absorbing their placidity, listening to their chewing, stroking their coats, warming in their body heat was, even for a young boy, a deeply nourishing experience.

The memory of my parents also sustains me. They were honest, upright, God-fearing and hardworking. They made many sacrifices for their children. Their example, their influence remains – and always will remain.

In the course of my work in radio it has been my privilege to meet extraordinary people whose example I could only aspire to, never reach... Gordon Wilson ('The bottom line is love'), Jean Vanier ('The poor evangelise us, they change us, if we let them touch our hearts...'). Then there are the kindnesses of ordinary people. A word or two of praise here, a gesture of affirmation there, a smile...

'O the grip, O the grip of irregular fields! No man
escapes'

(FROM 'THE GREAT HUNGER' BY PATRICK KAVANAGH)

*Neither is there escape from the sustenance of nature, whether it be
the fragile unfolding of a bud after a harsh wet winter or the majestic
solidity of a great beech tree, the wonder of its architecture and its
engineering feats. Truly Kilmer was right: 'Only God can make a
tree.' Likewise the rose, which in the words of medieval monk is
'without why':*

> The rose is without why
> She blooms because she blooms
> She does not care for herself
> Asks not if she is seen …

And I cannot leave out music. Mahler's powerful Resurrection
Symphony, *Allegri's* Miserere Mei, *a fragile cadence from a
Mozart concerto or a sweeping Tchaikowsky melody. All are food for
the soul.*

*Above all, the most direct sustenance of the spirit has to be the Mass.
I love its mystery, its communion. A day when I can fit the Mass
into the schedule is a truly special day. Failing that, a visit to
Donnybrook church sustains and nourishes like no other house of
God. Outside the traffic hurtles up and down one of Dublin's busiest
roadways, but within the great granite solidity of Donnybrook
church there is a calm and a reassuring peace that I have never
experienced elsewhere. If only to walk through it, I just love to be in
that place.*

*Enough! Reading back over this piece, it is almost frightening how
much of my spiritual sustenance comes out of 'that childhood
country'.*

> It was the garden of the golden apples,
> A long garden between a railway and a road,
> In the sow's rooting where the hen scratches
> We dipped our fingers in the pockets of God.

(FROM 'THE LONG GARDEN' BY PATRICK KAVANAGH)

John Quinn

Peace

And sometimes I am sorry when the grass
Is growing over the stones in quiet hollows
And the cocksfoot leans across the rutted cart-pass
That I am not the voice of country fellows
Who now are standing by some headland talking
Of turnips and potatoes or young corn
Or turf banks stripped for victory.
Here peace is still hawking
His coloured combs and scarves and beads of horn.
Upon a headland by a whiny hedge
A hare sits looking down a leaf-lapped furrow
There's an old plough upside-down on a weedy ridge
And someone is shouldering home a saddle-harrow.
Out of that childhood country what fools climb
To fight with tyrants Love and Life and Time?

PATRICK KAVANAGH (1904–67)

PAULINE BEWICK

For Marie Heaney

I have spent most of my life asking the WHY questions: If there is a God – Why are we here? – Why did he design us to be cruel? – Why did that wonderful person die of a disease? – Why, who, what can I blame or thank?...

My husband Pat said: 'Everything is an accident.' That relaxed my questioning and searching.

Richard Dawkins put it this way:

> ...nature is not cruel, only pitilessly indifferent. This is one of the hardest lessons for humans to learn. We cannot admit that things might be neither good nor evil, neither cruel nor kind, but simply callous – indifferent to all suffering, lacking all purpose.

> We humans have purpose on the brain. We find it hard to look at anything without wondering what it is 'for', what the motive for it is, or the purpose behind it... Show us almost any object or process, and it is hard for us to resist the 'Why' question.

I was left with no great conscious force to blame or thank for any wilful actions, which whittles it down to you and me, our own conscience, restraint, health, we can either do good or bad. We can look after our own health, be giving, can or can't commit suicide, but only to a limited extent do we have the power of choice. Nature is a huge force, it does not know why we make war, get diseases, enjoy sun, sex, intelligence, these happen because of a chain of natural events arrived at automatically, nature goes on and on. Or perhaps it is more of a comfort to believe Charles Handy's friend Kurt Vonnegut who said: 'We are here on earth to fart about, don't let anyone tell you different.'

Pauline Bewick

MICHAEL LONGLEY

Dear Marie

Thank you for your letter with its interesting request. I shall try to write about jazz which I love nearly as much as I love poetry. Sometimes I enjoy it more. I can remember the exact moment when the wonders of this music first grabbed me as a young boy. The English Number One tennis player, Tony Mottram, chose as one of his Desert Island Discs Fats Waller's 'Alligator Crawl'. I was standing in our kitchen at the time (early nineteen-fifties?), and thrilled to the rolling boogie bass of the great stride pianist. However, as an adolescent I first fell comprehensively in love with the romantic classics, Tchaikovsky, Rachmaninov, Chopin, Grieg. I continued to listen to jazz at school and then at Trinity College, Dublin, but my total conversion didn't come until I was twenty-five, the year I got married.

I discovered Sally Lipsitz's celebrated emporium in High Street, and in that dusty cubby-hole bought my first two LPs, Fats on the Air, *compilations of Fats Waller's radio work. I loved the drive, the warmth, the spontaneity, the insouciance, the dizzy humour, the weightless artistry of this hugely overweight man. To quote Louis Armstrong: 'Every time someone mentions Fats Waller's name, why you can see the grins on all the faces, as if to say, "Yeah, yeah, yeah, yeah, Fats is a solid sender, ain't he?"'*

Waller seamlessly combines sunniness and subversion, and can be very complicated indeed.

More than thirty years ago at a party in a friend's flat in Camden Street in Belfast the music was issuing from a tinny-sounding portable Dansette record player. I could just pick out through the crush and chatter a heartstopping voice, a rich contralto, one of the most majestic sounds in all music. The following day I rushed to Atlantic Records and asked for Bessie Smith albums. It is a miracle how backwoods keening – mainly by men – about sex and betrayal, money and hard times, was transformed by a few female singers with powerful voices into a universal lamentation, a sound that would encircle the globe. Bessie Smith was the greatest of them. I revere the intensity and pathos of her music, her courage and defiance, the elemental force of her personality.

My next hero was the legendary cornetist Bix Beiderbecke. He came from a white middle-class family who lived in Davenport on the Mississippi. As a teenager he listened to Bessie Smith, King Oliver, Louis Armstrong, and at the deepest level he took them all in. From the beginning his cornet sings out from the dimly recorded tum-te-tum throb of a youthful group called the Wolverines. To a modified Dixieland style he brought a lovely melodic line, a thrilling rhythmic propulsion, a note of sadness. Bix Beiderbecke was the first white man to play great jazz. My parents came from London to live in Belfast twelve years before I was born. In my twenties I wondered if I might be the first Englishman to write Irish poetry.

I went on to enjoy the music of Louis Armstrong, Jelly Roll Morton, Earl Hines, Coleman Hawkins, James P Johnston, Art Tatum, Ben Webster, Billie Holiday, Django Reinhardt, Count Basie, Duke Ellington and many more. I now buy jazz on CDs. Computer-enhanced and digitally remastered, seventy-year-old recordings sound as fresh as yesterday. Though my chief enthusiasm continues to be the jazz of the twenties and thirties, I recently fell in love with the quirky melodic lines of Thelonius Monk, a 'modernist'; and I have been reaching back to the beginning of the century and transcriptions from piano rolls of compositions by Scott Joplin and other ragtime composers. Jazz is huge.

That the suffering and degradation of slavery should bring forth so much redemptive beauty is miraculous. The spontaneity of this music must be one of the best antidotes against authoritarian systems that would tell us what to think and how to feel. I believe that its emergence in the century of the jackboot is of the greatest importance. Stalin hated it. The Nazis hated it. They were frightened of swing. Syncopation is the opposite of the goose-step. Perhaps jazz is our century's most significant contribution to the culture of the world.

May I have the next dance, Marie? Take it away!

Michael

TERRY PRONE

Dear Marie

When we moved into our first house, my new husband, Tom, brought a dozen cartons filled with everything from shoes to books. Opening one of the cartons containing books, I was thrilled to find a copy of Robert Bolt's play about Thomas More, A Man for All Seasons. *Thrilled because I had fallen in love with this work years before I met Tom, and there was something eerily pleasing about opening his copy and finding he had marked favourite passages which also happened to be my own favourites.*

What attracted us both to the saint as portrayed by Robert Bolt is that this was a successful and happy man. A member of the Establishment. An internationally recognised scholar. A friend of the King. A loving and beloved husband and father. He was the last man in the world you'd expect to die a martyr's death. He fell on no sword until that sword was inescapable. He used his brilliance and his subtlety to avoid becoming a hero, until nothing but his death would serve the circumstances of the time. Then, and only then, did he muster his courage to go to the scaffold, sure that his God 'will not refuse one who is so blithe to go to him'.

The play was first produced in 1961, and some years later was filmed, starring Paul Scofield as Sir Thomas More and Robert Shaw as Henry VIII. I've seen the film in the cinema eleven times and now have it on video, revisiting it (or the text) whenever I am frightened or saddened by life. There's always something in it to sustain – whether it is an insight about surviving treachery, about cowardice and courage, about family and friendship, about loneliness and loyalty.

My favourite section in the play is an encounter between More and the man who plans to marry his daughter, a dangerously simplistic enthusiast named Roper. Whenever a controversy threatens to overturn respect for the processes of law, I go back to it. At first glance, it's simply a lawyer talking law to an idealist. But it rewards re-reading, and demonstrates why another character in the play, describing him as both a scholar and a saint, goes on to say of More:

His scholarship is supported by his writings; saintliness is a quality less easy to establish. But from his wilful indifference to realities which were obvious to quite ordinary contemporaries, it seems all too probable that he had it…

Yours sincerely

Terry Prone

from *A Man For All Seasons*

MARGARET   Father, that man's bad.

MORE   There is no law against that.

ROPER   There is! God's law!

MORE   Then God can arrest him.

ROPER   Sophistication upon sophistication!

MORE   No, sheer simplicity. The law, Roper, the law. I know what's legal and not what's right. And I'll stick to what's legal.

ROPER   Then you set man's law above God's!

MORE   No, far below; but let *me* draw your attention to a fact – I'm not God. The currents and eddies of right and wrong, which you find such plain sailing, I can't navigate. I'm no voyager. But in the thickets of the law, oh, there I'm a forester. I doubt if there's a man alive who could follow me there, thank God…

(He says this last to himself)

ALICE *(Exasperated, pointing after RICH)*   While you talk, he's gone!

MORE   And go he should, if he was the Devil himself, until he broke the law!

ROPER   So now you'd give the Devil benefit of law!

MORE   Yes. What would you do? Cut a great road through the law to get after the Devil?

ROPER   I'd cut down every law in England to do that!

MORE *(Roused and excited)*   Oh? *(Advances on ROPER)* And
when the last law was down, and the Devil turned round on
you – where would you hide, Roper, the laws all being flat?
(He leaves him) This country's planted thick with laws from
coast to coast – man's laws, not God's – and if you cut them
down – and you're just the man to do it – d'you really think
you could stand upright in the winds that would blow then?
(Quietly) Yes, I'd give the Devil the benefit of law, for my own
safety's sake.

ROPER   I have long suspected this; this is the golden
calf; the law's your god.

MORE *(Wearily)*   Oh, Roper, you're a fool, God's my god...
(Rather bitterly) But I find him rather too *(Very bitterly)*
subtle... I don't know where he is nor what he wants.

ROSE DOYLE

Dear Marie

I really found it a puzzle to get together my thoughts on what I would, if ever I did, look to for spiritual guidance or even support. It made me realise how much I see and find the spiritual in the everyday things about me.

So – unable to come up with a definitive I'm sending you a few words each from William Blake and Ezra Pound – who wouldn't have had a thing in common, but then no-one has the exclusive on spiritual or any other kind of wisdom.

They're saying different things, of course, but then life is neither one thing nor another.

The Angel that presided o'er my birth
Said, 'Little creature form'd of Joy and Mirth,
'Go love without the help of Any Thing on Earth.'

WILLIAM BLAKE

What is the price of Experience? do men buy it for a song?
Or wisdom for a dance in the street? no, it is bought with the price
Of all that a man hath.

WILLIAM BLAKE

And the days are not full enough
And the nights are not full enough
And life slips by like a field mouse
Not shaking the grass.

EZRA POUND

The very best of luck with the book

Fond regards

Rose

AILBHE SMYTH

Dear Marie

Thank you for asking me to contribute to this book. I've had a lovely time over the past week or so, in the midst of this bleak winter, thinking about the myriad sources of spiritual sustenance there are for me in my life. And you're right, of course. Some of them are difficult to talk about, because they're so private or beyond the realm of language altogether. Still, I think that over the years poetry has been the most constant source of illumination and stillness for me. It's not that I read poetry consciously seeking spiritual balm, but sometimes, miraculously, when I least expect it, that is what I find there. I call it miraculous because I can't entirely explain why certain poems touch the core of my ordinary, familiar, human pain, and enable me to experience it completely. When that happens, there is a sense of profound healing, of '...this sweet/sensation of joy'.

I've chosen an extract from Elizabeth Bishop's wonderful poem 'The Moose' because it does exactly that. The moose is at one and the same time my own terror, my own grief and my understanding of them, for however brief a time.

Warm regards

Ailbhe Smyth

from The Moose

A moose has come out of
the impenetrable wood
and stands there, looms, rather,
in the middle of the road.
It approaches; it sniffs at
the bus's hot hood.

Towering, antlerless,
high as a church,
homely as a house
(or, safe as houses).
A man's voice assures us
'Perfectly harmless...'

Some of the passengers
exclaim in whispers,
childishly, softly,
'Sure are big creatures.'
'It's awful plain.'
'Look! It's a she!'

Taking her time,
she looks the bus over,
grand, otherworldly.
Why, why do we feel
(we all feel) this sweet
sensation of joy?

'Curious creatures,'
says our quiet driver,
rolling his r's.
'Look at that, would you.'
Then he shifts gears.
For a moment longer,

by craning backward,
the moose can be seen
on the moonlit macadam;
then there's a dim
smell of moose, an acrid
smell of gasoline.

ELIZABETH BISHOP (1911–79)

INDEX OF CONTRIBUTORS

INDEX OF SOURCES